Milton's Poetic Art

A Mask, Lycidas, and Paradise Lost

Milton's Poetic Art

A Mask, Lycidas, and Paradise Lost

John Reesing

Harvard University Press

Cambridge, Massachusetts

1968

For
Douglas Bush

Preface

This volume of essays includes discussions of three major poems by Milton: *A Mask Presented at Ludlow Castle* (popularly known as *Comus*), *Lycidas,* and *Paradise Lost.* My aim has been to see these works as complete artistic wholes, and in that way to contribute toward the general reassessment of Milton's poetic thought and art for which the scholarship of our century has been preparing the way.

The essays have been written during the last five years, in response to a variety of impulses: a wish to discover the answer to some question about theme or structure that has given me trouble in reading one or another of Milton's poems, or to resolve some controverted problem of interpretation, or to reply to some influential critical judgment that seemed to me mistaken. A certain amount of repetitiveness will almost inevitably manifest itself in studies produced for purposes so various and in a manner so unsystematic. Readers will nevertheless be able to feel, I hope, that the element of repetition has been reduced to a tolerable minimum. Such matters of the kind as remain will perhaps be regarded as continuities in theme and focus from which, despite variations in weight among the several essays, a more or less unified impression of the great poet may emerge.

Certain ideas about the influence of divine Providence upon human affairs, about man's proper role within the divine governance of things and his ultimate destiny, and about some fundamental implications of the Christian religion consistently stand out as belonging among Milton's deepest concerns. The source — or authority — for his ideas most frequently appealed to in these pages is the Bible. Often when one is puzzled by some difficulty of thought or expression in his poems, the Bible turns out to be the best source of help.

After that come the Greek and Latin classics, and then the literary tradition of Milton's native country (including always the most recent developments, with which he kept himself remarkably familiar). As for the technical aspects of his art as a poet, what chiefly stands out in these essays perhaps is praise for the rhythm. It has become unfashionable in our century to talk about the organ voice. Some readers have even felt that the ear of this poet, in his later years at least, was mechanical and crudely monotonous. My own experience of his verse differs totally, and I hope that the recurring enthusiasms of one enchanted listener may find some justification by persuading others to listen for that beauty. Not that a reduction in pleasure for the intellect is the price of enjoying Milton's music. That notion too, though so much favored in our time, strikes me as equally mistaken. In concert with an enlarging volume of analysis that has been appearing in recent years, these essays occasionally draw attention to the felicitous power Milton shows everywhere for expressing precise thought in melodious language.

Among standards of specifically critical doctrine, his fidelity to the principle of genre keeps turning up as a major implication of these studies. He never leaves any form exactly as he found it, to be sure. No major poet does. Neither, however, does a truly classical artist so radically alter any genre he works with as to distort its character, and Milton is always unfailingly classical.

In brief, the fundamental assumption behind all these essays is the familiar view of Milton as a classical-humanist-Christian poet of the English Renaissance. The following pages offer certain refinements of detail which have grown from that assumption and which in turn may provide additional support for it.

It will be obvious that I owe a great debt to the large company of Miltonists, whose labors have done so much to fit us for membership in the audience the poet desired. To one great monument of Miltonic scholarship I am continuously indebted. All quotations from Milton's writings are taken from the Columbia edition: *The Works of John Milton,* ed. Frank Allen Patterson et al., 18 vols. (New York, 1931–1938), which is referred to throughout as *Works.* The Bible (except in a few instances which are explicitly noted) is quoted from the Authorized Version, that document of scholarship and literary art which dates from Milton's own early childhood and which he came to know so well.

Most of my reading has been done at the Folger Shakespeare Library. I wish to thank the Director, Dr. Louis B. Wright, and all the members of his staff for many courtesies, which I have been enjoying now for a number of years. I should like also to express my gratitude to the directors and the staffs of various other libraries which, to my great profit and pleasure, I have had occasion to visit now and then in the course of my study for this volume: the Harvard College Library, the Milton S. Eisenhower Library in The Johns Hopkins University, the Library of Congress, the New York Public Library, the Boston Public Library, and the libraries of The Catholic University of America, the Washington Cathedral, the Protestant Episcopal Theological Seminary in Virginia (Alexandria), and the General Theological Seminary (New York).

Preface

A sabbatical leave granted by The George Washington University several years ago gave me leisure to begin the writing, and a grant from the University Committee on Research assisted with the expenses of preparing the manuscript for the press. Many friends here have forwarded my work by their encouragement and their helpful criticism. John A. Frey and John F. Latimer, respectively, checked and corrected my translations from French and Latin. I owe warm thanks also to my colleagues in the Department of English, who accorded a gracious and sympathetic hearing to "An Essay for the Tercentenary of *Paradise Lost*" when it was read before our Colloquium on 24 April 1967. More specifically, John G. Allee, Jr., Milton Crane, and Philip H. Highfill, Jr., have found time from their own pressing schedules to read one or another — or several — of the essays. Calvin D. Linton has read most of them and over the years has been a source of encouragement and of wise, learned counsel. All of these friends will recognize ways in which their good comments have helped to strengthen my work.

I am much indebted also to friends at other institutions. A. J. Carlson kindly responded to some questions about Elizabethan church history. Roland M. Frye read one of these studies, in an earlier and cruder form which his perspicacious comments helped to improve. For many years now my teacher and friend, Herschel Baker, has given generously of his time and learning in encouragement of my work, which here and in earlier studies owes more than I can say to his good offices, his criticism, and his example.

The book owes most of all to Douglas Bush, whose course in Milton opened my eyes to all manner of good things. Some parts of this volume he has seen, others he has not; but every page, though unworthy, is better for the influence of his scholarship, his guidance, and his friendship.

J. R.

Washington, D.C.
October 1967

Contents

Milton's Poetic Art

A Mask, Lycidas, and Paradise Lost

"Most Innocent Nature"

and

Milton's Ludlow 'Mask'

I

In the structure it developed under Ben Jonson's handling, the court masque has two main parts: (1) an antimasque, which sets up a problem and which makes a contrast with (2) the masque proper, which exhibits an ideal world, the world of harmony and order, therefore the world of permanence. Although professionals act and dance in the antimasque, the masque proper is performed by aristocratic persons disguised as gods and goddesses, or heroes. Thus it compliments the court, and as Stephen Orgel has recently shown, it characteristically moves toward the breaking down of the barrier between aristocratic performers and aristocratic spectators. When the Lady in Milton's Ludlow *Mask* begins to dance with the Lord President of Wales her father, and then others join in the dance, when performers and spectators thereby merge into one single community, the activity makes visible what has been assumed all along: the court *is* the ideal world. The court thus becomes what it contemplates, and the masque form fulfills its purpose as a didactic instrument of art.[1]

An imaginative form with such conventions as these must have seemed especially congenial to Milton,[2] for the conventions are so pleasingly congruous with certain major assumptions of his thought. Throughout his career he refers to Nature as a standard of pure and faultless morality. What he calls Nature is the perfect physico-moral order that he looks back to as the pristine historical reality, the whole creation as God originally made it. Although it is true that man's sin has vitiated this natural order, and also true that under grace the restoration of the corrupted order of nature has already begun, nevertheless Milton characteristically assumes the reality of something anterior to both situations — namely, perfect (i.e., unfallen) Nature. Only the latter is Nature properly so called, and only that which conforms to it as the norm is natural; to Nature in this

3

sense may be referred every moral question that can arise in the nature we inhabit, fallen nature.

Milton's explicit prose formulation of this set of ideas begins to develop in the 1640's, especially in the divorce tracts.[3] Later it appears in the *De Doctrina Christiana;* and *Paradise Lost,* especially in Books IV–VIII, develops an elaborate image of Nature. But before even the earliest of the controversial prose writings the ideas were appearing in the poems and college exercises,[4] and in 1634 they gave Milton the framework of assumptions philosophic and religious for his Ludlow *Mask.* In this essay I wish to suggest how convincingly the artistic coherence of the *Mask* reveals itself when we read it with these assumptions in mind.

As everybody feels, and as many readers have for long been objecting, the action is not seriously dramatic because the Lady is not attracted by Comus's solicitations; there is neither subtle characterization nor psychological complexity. But those qualities, virtues proper for serious drama, would be out of place here; one may grant the strictures and still regard them as virtues, not faults, in this work. For the Lady and her brothers belong to Nature in the sense defined above. She is an unfallen creature who sustains her position in an unfallen moral order that she calls natural. There also exists, of course, a fallen world of nature, to which most persons belong; Comus sees to that. But the Lady can desire nothing that he has to offer. In fact, all three of the young persons at the center of the *Mask's* action, since they belong to Nature, are triumphantly able not to feel drawn toward Comus's values; and indeed (the *Mask* is saying) all the members of the court, being truly "natural" persons, are similarly free.[5] The *Mask* so assumes partly because the masque is a mode of compliment, partly because to make the assumption is educative; to imagine for a while that we really are "natural" is a way of moving toward that desirable end.

4

"Most Innocent Nature"

The world of Nature to which all the members of the court are understood to belong is a world in which Ovidian transformations occur easily and commonly. The Nightingale (233–234, 565–566), Narcissus (236), Scylla (256), the "star of Arcady" (340), and Daphne (660–661) are among the mythological persons to whom apparently casual reference is made in the dialogue — apparently but not actually, because the references are there by design.[6] Nevertheless, such allusions are no more than harmonious embellishments, in keeping with the basic assumption and helpful for building up a solid texture of detail but peripheral to the chief idea.

Two main categories of transformation, which underlie respectively the antimasque and masque sections, may be identified as fundamental to the understanding of Milton's *Mask*. First and most obviously Comus, working in his mother's bad tradition, persuades men to drink a potion that unmans them (66–77). This, the basic assumption behind the action of the *Mask*, clearly derives from Ovid's poem. The other, opposite, kind of transformation may be illustrated from the Spirit's invocation to Sabrina. After the mention of six deities associated one way or another with the sea (Oceanus, Neptune, Tethys, Nereus, Proteus, Triton), we hear obsecrations to three mortals who have been metamorphosed into gods (Glaucus, Leucothea, and Melicertes: 873–875).[7] And Sabrina herself, though once a mortal, was "Made Goddess of the River" by "a quick immortal change," as the Spirit has already explained (840–841).[8]

Antimasque and masque set up a contrast between two opposite kinds of transformation open to human beings and determined for each person by the moral choices he makes: metamorphosis into a beast, or into a god. The idea is pervasively emphasized throughout the *Mask*, in a fusion of Ovidian, Platonic, and Christian materials extending from the Spirit's lines at the start about those who live "Unmindfull of the crown that

5

Vertue gives/After this mortal change, to her true Servants"
(9–10), through Elder Brother's eloquent version of the *Phaedo*
(452–474), to the enchanting invitation at the end:

> *Mortals that would follow me,*
> *Love vertue, she alone is free . . .*
> (1017–1018)[9]

We may say, then, that the *Mask* has to do with the relation of mortals to the world of the divine. Its theme is the moral
character of the timeless world of permanence and the moral
conditions for membership in it. Or, to state the idea another
way, the *Mask* is about the prospect of divinization open to all
human beings who live virtuously (i.e., according to Nature),
those who do not forget

> *. . . the crown that Vertue gives*
> *After this mortal change, to her true Servants*
> *Amongst the enthron'd gods on Sainted seats.*
> (9–11)[10]

This thesis, if true, will assure an affirmative answer to the
vexed question, Is Milton's Ludlow *Mask* truly a masque?[11]
Certainly it is possible to think of the Lady as a first sketch for
Eve because the work involves a favorite Miltonic theme, temptation — and that seems inappropriately dramatic for masque.
Nevertheless the young poet, working in a less pretentious form
than epic and one that has its own very different assumptions,
is not concentrating his imagination on a character in a fallen
world, who would be in need of redeeming grace and whose
contradictory motivations would invite a subtlety and complexity
of treatment out of place in the complimentary genre of masque.

He does intensify the seriousness of the dramatic element
and in that way modify the tradition, as we should expect;
Milton never leaves any genre just where he found it. As Orgel
has observed, this poet conceived "of a masque not as a court

ballet, but as a drama about the will" (p. 151). Yet for all its deepened intensities, the Ludlow *Mask* remains a masque; Milton, though certainly a very bold artist, is not a destructive one. Always he is classically obedient to the principles of genre. For his *Mask* conceived as a drama of the will he imagines an untroubled testing, and in that way a vindication, of the Lady's right to membership in the divine order of timeless permanence. "Mortal," "immortal," "human," "divine," "gods," "goddess," "eternal" are all key words. The Lady and her brothers, ultimately the whole court, are presented as members of a Nature that is believed to be the ideal moral order. By developing these assumptions Milton carries on the tradition of the Jonsonian masque, with the result that he involves the whole court in an idealized vision of itself and in that way makes his work conform to the standards of didactic compliment that Ben Jonson had taught a whole generation to expect in the court masque.[12]

II

We have the 1634 acting version of the *Mask*, in the Bridgewater MS.; the first printed version, of 1637; and presumably also, in the Trinity MS., the text both as Milton originally composed it, before it was trimmed for stage production, and as he revised it afterward.[13] The text in the Trinity MS., of course, has been so elaborately worked over that one cannot with every detail be sure of reconstructing the original composition. In any event, there are certain important aspects in which Trinity and 1637 agree but differ from Bridgewater: some features of the sequential pattern, and some matter omitted from Bridgewater but included in the others. When we consider the readings that Milton chose for the 1637 printing (and whether he was then bringing the text back to something like its original state, or changing the original state, or doing something of both), it would appear that two major categories of difference between 1637 and Bridgewater can be explained by reference to the theme as that has been expounded in the present essay.

(1) First is the dissatisfaction Milton seems to have felt with the Prologue and Epilogue of the acting version. In the arrangement for the stage production the Prologue was a twenty-line song for the Spirit,[14] who upon completing it began speaking, "Before the starrie threshold of Joves Courte," etc. The Trinity MS. made — but ultimately canceled — further amplification by adding after the fourth spoken line ("In regions milde of calm & serene Air") another passage of fourteen lines.[15] This extended description of a paradisal world, though beautiful in itself, does not quickly release its full thematic strength because we have not yet been given the perspective that would clearly reveal it. What we need to know is that we are hearing about a world of divinities that stands in some close and important relation with the world of mortal human beings. That perspective we receive when we begin to hear about "the smoak and stirr of this dim spot,/Which men call Earth"; and for 1637 Milton found the most efficient place for it. What had been lines 25–26 in Bridgewater, and 19–20 in Trinity, in 1637 appeared as lines 5–6.

The short Epilogue of the acting version was as inefficient in its way as the Prologue had been: six lines of description, not very evocative and not profoundly relevant, followed by the didactic incantation, "mortalls that would follow me," etc. Milton's ultimate solution was to use these twelve lines as the conclusion (now 1011–1022) for an Epilogue four times the length in Bridgewater, enlarged as follows:

(a) by returning to their apparently original position, with appropriate modifications, nineteen of the twenty lines from the Bridgewater Prologue (now 975–982, 987–995, 997–998);
(b) and by enlarging this group of nineteen lines with seventeen new ones (983–986, 996, 999–1010).

The result is to give to a brilliantly evocative description of the Spirit's paradise the most effective position possible, a position *after* everything we have been hearing about gods and men, metamorphosis and immortality and divinity. Also we hear about two additional mortals famous in myth as having been transformed into gods: Adonis and Psyche.

(2) Milton seems also to have wished the printed text of the *Mask* to possess the fullness of "Christian coloring" that presumably he had given to his work to start with. Certainly the Bridgewater text is an explicitly Christian work (11, 418, 452, 1022 — to use our line numbering). The additional Christian passages appearing in both Trinity and 1637 but not in the acting version are an image in the Lady's first scene (187–189) and the passage about her vision of Faith, Hope, and Chastity (212–214). Then the most striking of all the Christian items, absent from both Bridgewater and Trinity and new in 1637, comes in the passage about "the sage/And serious doctrine of Virginity," lines in which the Lady raises the argument from the level of natural reason to that of revealed religion (779–798).[16]

At least one major purpose of all these Christian passages that Milton restored or added for 1637 is, I suggest, to mute the Pelagian overtones that might be sensed in the work. The *Mask* assumes that the virtuous are the truly natural, that Virtue is the condition for membership in the order of Nature and for advancement to divine status "After this mortal change." But this very assumption, on which the entire work rests and by which it is able to exercise its complimentary and didactic influence upon all the members of the Lord President's court, may itself suggest that the Virtue by which good persons will win a place in heaven is theirs by right, on their own.[17] And indeed there are three particular items which have been present from the earliest version and which, though easily susceptible of

orthodox Christian interpretation, *might* be understood as im-
plying a certain Pelagian notion of self-sufficiency. Each of the
following can be read as denying, or at least as slighting, the
fundamental principle that grace is absolutely necessary for all
creatures (even unfallen ones) who aspire to attain a heavenly
status.

(a) *Yet som there be that by due steps aspire*
 To lay their just hands on that Golden Key
 That ope's the Palace of Eternity:
  (12–14)

(b) *2 Bro. What hidden strength,*
 Unless the strength of Heav'n, if you mean that?
  Eld. Bro. I mean that too, but yet a hidden strength
 Which if Heav'n gave it, may be term'd her own:
  (415–418)

(c) *Mortals that would follow me,*
 Love vertue, she alone is free,
 She can teach ye how to clime
 Higher then the Spheary chime;
 Or if Vertue feeble were,
 Heav'n it self would stoop to her.
  (1017–1022)

Milton would surely not be slow to sense the possible Pelagian
tendencies of these lines, especially within the context of the
basic assumption made by the *Mask*. From such a premise we
may conclude that he was trying (perhaps among several purposes) to eliminate the Pelagian overtones when he increased
the strength of the Christian notes for the printed version of
1637.

Hence (in part) the connection the Lady makes between
chastity and charity.[18] The relation is relevant to a very different
kind of problem that has been expressed by many readers in our
time. The Chastity celebrated by the Ludlow *Mask* has been

felt to be simply negative, and the Lady's moral attitude has
been disliked as proceeding from an austerity mechanical and
merely self-regarding. In fact, her moral attitude is truly positive
and outgoing. She is virtuous because she loves the Good — or,
in the vocabulary of Christian theology, she loves God with the
infused love of divine charity.

Christian Chastity is a mode of Temperance. Christian
Temperance sets limits to the indulgence of all sensuous pleasures and in certain circumstances says "No" to some, not because
it thinks sensuous pleasures bad (Temperance knows they are
good in themselves),[19] and not simply in order to love God
(though that is part of its motive), but because it already loves
Him; Temperance wants to go on loving God. The Chastity
celebrated in this *Mask* is a purity of soul that both helps to
make possible, and in turn is enhanced by, love of God. The
passage about the Lady's vision of Faith, Hope, and Chastity
reveals her as giving herself in love to the Supreme Good. It
serves to objectify for one moment in the dramatic action the
continuous moral and religious basis of her entire life; and also
by dramatizing her responsiveness to spiritual reality it may
enhance our own emotional sympathy for her and for the virtue
being celebrated in the *Mask*.[20]

In the manner of a good Renaissance poet, Milton can
bring together within a space of five lines materials from Christian and classical sources (Faith, Hope, Chastity; "he, the Supreme good" — 212–216), or can fuse such materials within a
single line ("Amongst the enthron'd gods on Sainted seats" —
11). The presence of Christian materials here and elsewhere
throughout the *Mask* obviously implies that familiar Christian
ideas about grace are being assumed. However, neither in this
work nor anywhere else in his verse or prose does Milton carefully analyze (in the manner of a Scholastic theologian, say)
the exact areas proper respectively to natural reason and super-

natural grace. He always finds it more congenial to think rather, in a concrete and unanalyzed way, of one single order, the perfect physico-moral order which he understands God to have created in the beginning and to have endowed with grace. Of course he knows the distinction between nature and grace, but his characteristic way of thinking about them is unanalytically to postulate the fusion of them in one concrete actuality.[21] That is the Nature which the Lady defends, the Nature to whose order she belongs and to which, under the *donnée* assumed by the *Mask*, all the members of the court belong. By love, and action inspired by such love, the Lady participates in the perfect moral order of Nature. Her virtue, in this sense, will ultimately open for her the Palace of Eternity.

III

This essay will have occasioned no surprise by asserting that in 1634 Milton devised for his Ludlow *Mask* a story about the interaction of gods and mortals; he had already been using related ideas for some years. In his earlier poems, and in his college exercises, he had often written about the relation between earth and heaven, indeed about the community between gods and men, the human and the divine. Both of the two important poems of 1629 (the fifth Latin *Elegy* and the *Nativity Hymn*) take that subject for their theme, in their respective ways; and similar ideas appear, sometimes more cursorily, in the prose and verse writings of the early 1630's.[22] Nevertheless, congenial as the whole set of ideas obviously was to Milton from the first, his allegorical mode of handling it in the *Mask* has often left readers puzzled in certain ways.

For one thing, it is sometimes hard to say where literal meaning ends and allegorical meaning begins. The visible disfigurement wrought by Comus's magic drink obviously allegorizes a deformation of the moral personality; in refusing the potion the Lady certainly is resisting his assault upon her will, and successfully. But how should we interpret her imprisonment in the magic chair, which continues even after Comus and his crew have been forced to withdraw? Is it an allegory for some immobilizing power that evil may have over good? Or does it mean the simple literal fact which the Lady herself states, that "this corporal rinde/Thou has immancl'd, while Heav'n sees good" (663–664)?

It means both, I should suppose. The *Mask* is saying that, in this world, innocent goodness may sometimes be trapped and imprisoned by superhuman powers of evil, and that human goodness can escape only if it is delivered by some superhuman good. Good impulses, even good actions, may be neutralized; good persons may be attacked by slander; their bodies may be imprisoned, injured, or killed. Milton certainly believes that the spiritual forces of wickedness have the power to bring any and all of these things to pass. When the Lady sits immobile in Comus's magic chair, she is presenting an allegorical picture of the invisible influence that evil can wield, and at the same time literally suffering the physical limitation that we see.[23]

This complexity may or may not represent an imperfection in Milton's allegorical technique. His technique with two other allegorical symbols, however, would seem to be less than perfectly successful because it leaves the meaning of the symbols unclear. Haemony, since it is "more med'cinal . . . then that *Moly*/That *Hermes* once to wise *Ulysses* gave" (635–636), must be something superior to rational temperance,[24] and the only thing higher than reason is grace. And yet, as Douglas Bush has noted, "if it were religious faith or divine grace, its efficacy would surely be less limited than it proves to be." [25] Again, Sabrina presumably signifies something greater than haemony, but how can that be possible if grace has already been introduced under the symbol of haemony? But suppose that

Sabrina does represent grace. Obviously the Lady already knows about grace, and possesses it, and loves it (212–224). Obviously, too, she is chaste; and apparently, to judge from her lines about "the sage/And serious doctrine of Virginity" (778–798), she knows specifically about the revealed motive for chastity.[26] Nevertheless, she remains trapped in Comus's magic chair until Sabrina comes to her rescue. What precisely can Sabrina bestow that the Lady does not already possess?

We may solve these problems, I believe, by considering three types of information we are given about haemony.

(1) According to the Spirit, haemony has enabled him to do two things: to see through Comus's disguise, and to enter his presence invulnerable to any paralyzing enchantment (643–646).

(2) It is a plant which nobody honors here but which "in another Countrey" bears "a bright golden flowre" (630–634).

(3) It is introduced under an image of martial armor:

> Alas good ventrous youth,
> I love thy courage yet, and bold Emprise,
> But here thy sword can do thee little stead,
> Far other arms, and other weapons must
> Be those that quell the might of hellish charms.
> (608–612)

Now these lines may remind us of a passage in the sixth chapter of Ephesians which, though irrelevant (as I believe) for explaining the famous crux in *Lycidas*,[27] is able to help us interpret haemony:

Finally then, find your strength in the Lord, in his mighty power. Put on all the armour which God provides, so that you may be able to stand firm against the devices of the devil. For our fight is not against human foes, but against cosmic powers, against the authorities and potentates of this dark world, against the superhuman forces of evil in the heavens. Therefore, take up

God's armour; then you will be able to stand your ground when things are at their worst, to complete every task and still to stand. Stand firm, I say. Buckle on the belt of truth; for coat of mail put on integrity; let the shoes on your feet be the gospel of peace, to give you firm footing; and, with all these, take up the great shield of faith, with which you will be able to quench all the flaming arrows of the evil one. Take salvation for helmet; for sword, take that which the Spirit gives you — the words that come from God. (Eph. vi.10–17)[28]

Surely we may think of Comus as one among the evil "cosmic powers," as a representative of "the superhuman forces of evil in the heavens" (or of "spiritual wickedness in high places," as the more familiar Authorized Version has it). If so, the Christian reverberations of 608–612 may confirm the impression given in 630–634: when the Spirit says that haemony is a plant ill-esteemed here, he is referring to the universal accessibility of divine grace, and the general human neglect of it.

I should conclude that haemony is not divine grace *simpliciter* but that its symbolic meaning certainly involves the idea of grace. Perhaps, as Bush suggests, it "represents Platonic-Christian temperance. . . ."[29] Or perhaps a more inclusive term may be preferred. Could haemony be Christian virtue in general?[30] Or perhaps it represents the spiritual armor by which a Christian is enabled to combat "the superhuman forces of evil in the heavens." If anyone asks why spiritual armor should be symbolized by a plant, I should have to reply that the "armor of God" in Ephesians vi is clearly a divine aid against super-human powers of evil, that haemony is explicitly represented as such (611–612, 629, 643–648), and that presumably Milton is transposing a martial image into a mode appropriate for pastoral masque.[31]

Any of these interpretations would be congruent with the explicit language of the *Mask*. Since all of them involve the idea of divine assistance as appropriated by human beings for human action, all will accommodate the fact that men, being men, may fail even when divinely aided. All would therefore do justice to the fact that the boys fail to rescue their sister even though they possess the divine assistance of haemony. And hence any of the three interpretations would make it possible for us to understand that Sabrina represents something still higher. We might interpret Sabrina as divine grace without reference to any limits upon its operation brought about by human frailty — either grace *simpliciter,* or as Bush has suggested more particularly (and perhaps preferably), "the divine grace that must reinforce rational temperance." [32]

With any of these related interpretations we may bring the symbolic significance of Sabrina into relation with one of Milton's most important Christian insights. Despite the fact that masque is a genre for compliment, the Lady's brothers are allowed to fail. Though armed with divine protection, they succeed merely in driving Comus away; they do not defeat his power. That is reserved for a divine person, actually present. Milton believes that man's proper role is, in an attitude of complete dependence upon God, to respond to the situations with which a benevolent Providence confronts him, content to endure any peril "while Heav'n sees good" (664), confident that in due course Heaven will provide whatever is needed, defense or rescue. If the brothers had succeeded in carrying out the Spirit's full instructions (646–655), it might have appeared that human beings, albeit with divine aid, were winning the victory over evil. Whereas in the long run nothing but divine rescue will save man from the power of evil because the only power able to defeat evil is God. So, from whatever combination of motives, Milton is working with a story that is congruent with his deepest Christian impulses. As things in fact work out, the Lady remains helpless until she is rescued, and rescued by nothing less than a divine power. If it is only a lesser divinity who accomplishes the

rescue, and if the Lady's need for it is significantly different
from Adam's, nevertheless the rescue effected by Sabrina occurs
by the will of high Jove. The Lady has been endowed with
grace from the beginning, to be sure. But then, grace is something that mortals need continuously, and no one can receive too
much of it. May we conclude that Sabrina makes possible, or
mediates, or confers, a new effusion of divine grace upon the
Lady in her desperate need, to rescue her from an otherwise
irremediable disaster? [33]

Two bits of evidence may help to confirm the general
tendency of this interpretation. The first involves a difference
between the acting text and the other versions. In the Bridgewater MS. the lines between Sabrina's disappearance and the
entrance of the country dancers (921–956) are divided between
the Spirit and the Elder Brother; Trinity and 1637 assign them
to the Spirit alone. Thus in the acting version Elder Brother
has line 937 ("Come sister while heav'n lends us grace"), by
which, at the very least, some general connection between
Sabrina and grace may be suggested. But 1637, by reassigning
the line to the Spirit ("Com Lady while Heaven lends us
grace"), arranges that the idea should come before readers with
very much higher authority. And secondly, we may remember
the fact already noted in an earlier section, that Milton apparently felt it desirable to intensify the Christian notes when he
was preparing the text for printing in 1637. Though he made
no direct substantive changes in the details of the text concerning haemony and Sabrina themselves, perhaps one of his aims
in restoring and deepening the Christian notes earlier in the
Mask had been to provide a more decisively Christian ambience
for those two symbols, and thereby to guide us toward a right
understanding of them.

Obviously this essay has worked from the premise that the
difficulties many readers have felt with the *Mask* are actually

there. The uncertainties about the allegory are more than pseudo-problems, and I believe it must be acknowledged that Milton's allegorical technique is not faultless. Still, one may feel that the ultimate result is something for which "failure" is hardly an appropriate word.[34] The problems result from defects not of coherence but of clarity.

With respect to the coherence of its artistic purpose, theme, and decorum, the *Mask* seems to me triumphantly successful. Even for the problems with certain details in the allegory we are given enough light to let us perceive the coherence of their relation to everything else. The interpretations of haemony and of Sabrina offered above are congruent with the thesis developed earlier in this essay, that the *Mask* dramatizes the relation between mortals and the world of divinities. Certainly the thesis receives support from plot and characterization, rudimentary as they must necessarily be in the undramatic genre of masque. And even the verbal texture — perhaps one should say, especially the verbal texture — supports it. To be unpoetically schematic for a moment, a very small number of categories will account for virtually every phrase of the text: the divine world of the gods, the temporal world of mortals, the relation between the two orders, the dehumanizing metamorphosis of human beings, or their deification. Reading through the work with a knowledge of its key assumption, one is struck by the integrity of the imagination at work in it. In its final state the *Mask* has acquired a wonderfully cohesive fusion of all its varied materials, and in the successive versions of the text that have come down to us we can observe Milton's impulse toward imaginative integrity gradually realizing itself.

Justice for Lycidas

Lycidas, whatever its universal implications may ultimately be, is in the first instance a poem about Lycidas; and the questioning of divine justice occasioned by that young shepherd's premature and violent death is not allayed until the last paragraph of the speaker's memorial verses. How he comes to his confident assurance that all is well (165–185), so suddenly after his most intense and agonized protest against cosmic injustice (154–164), is the first topic I wish to discuss. Certain details of the speaker's imagery can tell us much about the dramatic progress of his thought and feeling, and also about the meaning of the justice for Lycidas that he finally perceives.

The complaint against injustice to Lycidas is expressed in a way that shows the speaker to be thinking about himself as well as about his lost friend. Meanwhile, such comfort as is offered in the speech by Phoebus (76–84) does not really come to grips with the problem about Lycidas. Phoebus' words say nothing about what is happening to Lycidas now, and they offer no assurance at all that affairs are governed justly in *this* world. Even about the next world they are tantalizingly ambiguous. Does Phoebus mean that the virtuous will live in heaven personally enjoying the fame they deserve, or only that the immortal gods will forever know the merits of the virtuous, the virtuous themselves having perished? The speech is ambiguous at precisely the point where classical antiquity itself is uncertain; Milton could hardly have found a more illuminating way to suggest the inadequacies of the classical tradition.

So the speaker is not really comforted, and he is soon falling back sullenly into the blindest kind of superstitious paganism:

> It was that fatal and perfidious Bark
> Built in th' eclipse, and rigg'd with curses dark,
> That sunk so low that sacred head of thine.
> (100–102)

Neptune's Herald has already confessed his failure to understand (91–92); and the representative of learning comes with nothing more than a question, which goes simply unanswered (107). Then St. Peter replies, not to the speaker's complaint, but to his own. His answer, though it darkly affirms that an irresistible power will bring the bad shepherds to justice, offers nothing to assuage grief for the loss of Lycidas, and nothing to suggest any ultimate justice for him personally. Obviously the saint's threat of retribution to the wicked fails to still the speaker's questioning, which, notwithstanding the little ease falsely surmised in the flower passage, returns at its most intense in lines 154–164 ("Ay me! Whilst thee the shores, and sounding Seas").[1] Thus, in spite of everything he hears, the speaker's own thought moves persistently toward an agonized vision of blank mindlessness in a universe of mere physical force, where Lycidas' body is perhaps hurled to "the bottom of the monstrous world" (158).

Here, then, we meet the question from which we began. How can the speaker shift so suddenly to the consolation, "Weep no more, woful Shepherds weep no more" (165)? Granted that the literary tradition Milton is following sanctions, and calls for, the shift, is there anything in the psychological pattern of this speaker's experience that can justify so startling an about-turn?

The answer, I suggest, is to be found in some of the words the speaker himself uses in his climactic statement of the problem. In focusing successively on the loss to art, to learning, and to religion, the poem has suggested, through a series of gradually expanding images, that each of these human endeavors is cultivated in a community — a community of shepherds who are poets, who are scholars, who are also priests.[2] In the climactic passage, at the moment when the community is being sensed as national, patriotic feelings are themselves caught up into a

22

still larger awareness of cosmic order, while at the same time
the very existence of cosmic order is being questioned:

> *Ay me! Whilst thee the shores, and sounding Seas*
> *Wash far away, where ere thy bones are hurl'd,*
> *Whether beyond the stormy* Hebrides
> *Where thou perhaps under the whelming tide*
> *Visit'st the bottom of the monstrous world;*
> *Or whether thou to our moist vows deny'd,*
> *Sleep'st by the fable of* Bellerus *old,*
> *Where the great vision of the guarded Mount*
> *Looks toward* Namancos *and* Bayona's *hold;*
> *Look homeward Angel now, and melt with ruth.*
> *And, O ye* Dolphins, *waft the haples youth.*
> (154–164)

The image of the community has been developed partly by
the speaker, partly by Phoebus, Camus, and St. Peter. Now
the uncouth swain himself speaks words that expand the image
to the grandest proportions it has so far achieved. But in
voicing his climactic indictment — that the world is governed,
not blindly, but not at all; that reality is, not merely irrational
or deliberately malevolent, but totally mindless — he uses, without at first quite grasping their significance, words that assert
the opposite: a real seeing ("the great vision," "Looks,"
"Look") and a providential care ("the guarded Mount"). Also
his words about Lycidas ("Visit'st," "Sleep'st") interject into
this picture of mindless, mechanical force a softening note of
humanity. And so he suddenly does begin to understand, because he himself has spoken words that open his mind to the
sources of consolation. It takes only a moment for the full
meaning of his words to flash before him. Then the turn begins
at once without a pause, *sotto voce* at first as the truth of what
he has known all along begins to take possession of him, rising
quickly to the exultation of "Flames in the forehead of the
morning sky" (171), then gradually leveling out with the vision

23

of a greater pastoral order in heaven, and finally of a new harmony between heaven and earth.

Thus is made possible for him a completely satisfying vision, which he both receives and expresses in images of Christian pastoral. For this shepherd has known the Christian promises all along, though his faith in them has been bitterly strained. Milton, writing in anno Domini 1637, here as always remembers that he has been graced to live after the Incarnation, in the full light of revelation. The world has moved on since Theocritus and Virgil. Of course it is *Christian* pastoral that Milton writes; and characteristically he transforms the tradition. "A Faith on Trial": the precisely accurate words of Douglas Bush[3] point us to the main source of tension in the poem. *Lycidas* dramatizes the agony of a shepherd whose Christian faith is strained almost to the breaking point and who, without at first seeing what he is doing, finds his way back to the life of faith.[4]

II

Some implications of certain details in the speaker's last paragraph may now be explored. With St. Peter's speech the poem has moved from an answer that is at least verbally classical to one that is explicitly Christian.[5] The latter cannot satisfy completely, however, because it ends with thoughts of vengeance rather than of redemption; its organization of Christian insights, thus imperfectly balanced, obviously cannot be final. But in his last paragraph the speaker achieves a vision that does console, and in developing it he uses nearly everything that has gone before, transposed now into a new key.

Christ is everywhere in the last paragraph, but always indirectly. The "smite" of line 131, with its note of merciless vengeance, is recalled by "might" in 173, the tone of which is qualified by suggestions of bravery and triumphant strength in "dear" already set in motion by the splendid sun image of 168–171.[6] Thereby is added to the pastoral dominant throughout the poem, and to the sense of Christ as shepherd, king, and avenging judge, the new note of a mighty and victorious hero. Then for line 181 ("And wipe the tears for ever from his eyes") Milton remembers a verse from the Apocalypse that brings both the pastoral and the kingly into association with feelings of tenderness and redemption and self-offering: "For the Lamb which is in the midst of the throne shall feed them, and shall lead them unto living fountains of waters: and God shall wipe away all tears from their eyes" (Rev. vii.17). This verse makes it possible for line 181 to agitate reverberations from many earlier parts of the poem. "For the Lamb . . . shall feed them" counterbalances "The hungry Sheep look up, and are not fed" (125), with its ironic allusion to John xxi.15–17.[7] Also we may see line 181 as bringing into focus a long process of thought and feeling about justice, a process that has already moved from Phoebus' vision of "all-judging *Jove*" to St. Peter's implicitly pastoral image of Christ as the just Judge.[8] "And wipe the tears for ever from his eyes," by recalling Rev. vii.17, completes the theme of the perfect Shepherd-Judge-King. Thus is transmuted all the fierceness of 130–131.

Now at last the speaker perceives the role that divine justice has called Lycidas to assume. In some mysterious way heavenly fields have been united with earthly ones in a new and richer harmony than has existed before — apparently because Lycidas has passed through death.

> *Now* Lycidas *the Shepherds weep no more;*
> *Henceforth thou art the Genius of the shore,*
> *In thy large recompense, and shalt be good*
> *To all that wander in that perilous flood.*
> (182–185)

25

We know from the rhythm that this answer to the question of God's justice truly consoles. The last line of Phoebus' speech, where cadence so totally coincides with the iambic pattern, has given an impression of mechanical patness,[9] and of course St. Peter's last words were obviously no stopping place. But the supple cadences of the true answer play against the iambic norm with a fresh and subtle beauty, and the effect is enhanced by similarities of sound that bring three important words into association: *"Lycidas,"* "Genius," "perilous."

Still, mystery remains. The poem does not answer the question, Why? It does develop its own version of that favorite Miltonic theme, the amazing creativity of God, which is always acting redemptively to bring a new and greater good out of discord and evil. Divine justice, although mysteriously it permits suffering and loss, is nevertheless an overflowing generosity, and is therefore endlessly surprising, even to saints. Peter himself has supposed that Lycidas was born to shepherd a diocese; whereas the chief Shepherd has had greater things in mind. The speaker has moved from the slightest conception of reward possible (12–14), through a desolating fear that there shall be no rewards at all (73–76), and the sternly calculating attitudes of Phoebus and St. Peter (83–84, 130–131), to this vision of "large recompense," with its suggestions of divine mercy and generosity. And yet, for all that, the idea of "justice" is not dropped; "recompense" comes from *pendere*.

"Engine" and "Genius," too, have a significant etymological link, since both derive from *ingenium*. The early suggestions of purposelessness are absorbed, with "engine," into opposite suggestions of intelligent contrivance, which in turn are enlarged and softened by "Genius" — already influenced by "dear might" — into a sense of benevolent personality. Ultimately the two words go back to *gignere* and so, in this lament for a dead shepherd, learnedly underscore hints of life. Lines 183–185 perfectly answer the earlier lines about Nature's sorrow (37–49); and with "Genius" we remember, too, the emphasis in "Sheep-hook" (120), that instrument and symbol of pastoral office which the false shepherds have not learned to hold. *This* shepherd will "be good/To all that wander in that perilous flood." And not for religious values only. Learning and poetry, too, have a future in the world; "shore" and "flood" take us back to earlier moments when, with very different feelings, we were thinking about Orpheus, Theocritus, and Virgil (58–63, 85–86).[10]

Indeed, we shall not exaggerate if we say that everything we have been hearing is totally present, in a new way, in the speaker's last four lines. That is the kind of poet Milton had learned to be by the time he was approaching his twenty-ninth birthday; he was able to fuse everything. Obviously we shall not come to the end of the felicities of detail in this miraculous poem; all the more reason for wishing to identify the principle of its total order. That, as with any poem, must be the action of sensibility, which in responding to everything holds all its multiple energies together. What from this point of view gives *Lycidas* the distinguishing quality we all recognize is, I suggest, a uniquely Miltonic blend of poignance and outrage. The first is proper to the man with a strong sense that life is, specifically, *sweet,* such a sense as Adam expresses in his phrase "the sweet of Life" and in the whole delicious passage where it occurs (*P.L.* VIII.180–197). In *Lycidas* this keen sense of life's sweetness is everywhere in the rhythm, and occasionally explicit in the imagery (6, 39–48, 134–151, 175, 179). Outrage, which depends on a strong sense for order, is also everywhere in the poem, in imagery, rhythm, tempo, and volume; and everywhere it is qualified by the poignance.

For the speaker the vision of justice for Lycidas dissolves all the grounds of protest. For the poem itself the painful tensions are resolved through the quiet impersonality of a third-

27

person perspective in the *ottava rima* stanza at the end, for which Milton imagines another, anonymous, voice, with a more predictably regular pattern of rhythm and rhyme. Images of sound and light and gesture recall earlier, agonized, moments, as in line after line they quietly affirm a recovered sense of order and meaning in life. All the earlier scenes on earth and in heaven come together in the golden prospect of line 190, poised and yet bursting with promise of new life ("And now the Sun had stretch'd out all the hills"). By that and the three lines that follow, the energies of poignance and outrage are finally reorganized into a serene perception of the physical world as a divine order in which, despite its manifold dangers, man may strive toward his ideals in confidence and hope.

The Decorum of St. Peter's Speech in 'Lycidas'

I

This essay must begin with a fair warning: it is about the two-handed engine. Perhaps readers may be persuaded to endure yet another discussion of the old problem if they are offered two comments. It was attention to some other sections of *Lycidas*[1] that led me into the study for the present essay,[2] and the interpretation I shall propose for lines 130–131 holds some promise of enhancing our enjoyment and appreciation of Milton's art in general.

One firm principle may guide us into the problem. Decorum, which for Milton is always "the grand master-piece to observe,"[3] suggests that the two-handed engine must surely be something that we can associate both with shepherds and with bishops, who are Christian shepherds. We may feel, too, with the majority of interpreters, that the source is Biblical. The twenty-third Psalm gives us the clue — "thy rod and thy staff they comfort me"; and a glance at the concordance turns up a longer passage, the tenth chapter of Isaiah, in which images of rod and staff conspicuously recur, along with images of smiting.

Like St. Peter, whose threat of the two-handed engine is at once bad news for the wicked shepherds and good news for the righteous ones, Isaiah makes an interestingly ambivalent use of his imagery. At first, rod and staff symbolize, quite simply, the anger of God, who uses the Assyrian to chastise Israel:

O Assyrian, the rod of mine anger, and the staff in their hand is mine indignation. I will send him against an hypocritical nation, and against the people of my wrath will I give him a charge, to take the spoil, and to take the prey, and to tread them down like the mire of the streets. (vv. 5–6)

Nevertheless, the Assyrian is himself not guiltless, and a remnant of Israel will return:

And it shall come to pass in that day, that the remnant of Israel, and such as are escaped of the house of Jacob, shall no more again stay upon him that smote them; but shall stay upon the Lord, the Holy One of Israel, in truth. The remnant shall return, even the remnant of Jacob, unto the mighty God. (vv. 20–21)

Therefore the people of God are not to fear, Isaiah reasons (vv. 24–25), and begins to change the tone of his key images:

Therefore thus saith the Lord God of hosts, O my people that dwellest in Zion, be not afraid of the Assyrian: he shall smite thee with a rod, and shall lift up his staff against thee, after the manner of Egypt. For yet a very little while, and the indignation shall cease, and mine anger in their destruction. And the Lord of hosts shall stir up a scourge for him according to the slaughter of Midian at the rock of Oreb: and as his rod was upon the sea, so shall he lift it up after the manner of Egypt. And it shall come to pass in that day, that his burden shall be taken away from off thy shoulder, and his yoke from off thy neck, and the yoke shall be destroyed because of the anointing. (vv. 24–27)[4]

In one chapter the multivalent image of the rod comes to symbolize a divine power that in a single act works vengeance upon the wicked and deliverance for the faithful: the Assyrians' rod, Pharaoh's rod, is mastered by the rod of the Lord of hosts.

In the course of the Bible as a whole the rod takes on a multiplicity of meanings and associations,[5] nearly all of which Milton seems to have in mind as he makes his image of the two-handed engine. The rod of Moses, the first shepherd of Israel, will always suggest, among other things, that triumphant deliverance when the children of Israel went "on dry ground through the midst of the sea" (Ex. xiv.16, 27).[6] The Biblical rod can suggest terrible vengeance, but it can also reassure: "thy rod [*shebet*] and thy staff [*misheneth*] they comfort me." [7] It can symbolize the authority possessed by a shepherd, and the order a good shepherd maintains as he governs his flock (Lev. xxvii.32 — *shebet*). It can symbolize the authority and power of kingly rule, in particular the sovereignty of Christ the King of

Kings, who will rule the nations "with a rod of iron" (Rev. xix.15 — *ῥάβδος*; cf. Rev. ii.27, xii.5; Ps. ii.9 — *shebet,* cx.2 — *matteh).* It symbolizes the Christ Himself: Isaiah begins his eleventh chapter with the words, "And there shall come forth a rod [*choter*] out of the stem of Jesse." Jesus, "that great shepherd of the sheep" (Heb. xiii.20), is a descendant of David, the shepherd-king (1 Sam. xvi–xvii).

Jesus' parable of the Last Judgment, which combines royal imagery with pastoral, reminds us of the shepherd's rod; and it is, I believe to the rod suggested in the words italicized below (v. 32) that the famous crux in *Lycidas* is referring:

> When the Son of man shall come in his glory, and all the holy angels with him, then shall he sit upon the throne of his glory: And before him shall be gathered all nations; *and he shall separate them one from another, as a shepherd divideth his sheep from the goats:* And he shall set the sheep on his right hand, but the goats on the left. Then shall the King say unto them on his right hand . . . Then shall he say also unto them on the left hand . . . (Matt. xxv.31–41)[8]

The parable tends to fuse three of the great Biblical images for Christ (in the Psalms, and elsewhere): Shepherd, Judge, and King. Of the two latter another example, especially interesting for our purposes, appears in Hebrews i.8: "But unto the Son he saith, Thy throne, O God, is for ever and ever: a sceptre of righteousness is the sceptre of thy kingdom." Here, where the writer is quoting Psalm xlv.6, the word for "sceptre," *ῥάβδος,* is the same as that used elsewhere in the New Testament for "rod" (1 Cor. iv.21; Heb. ix.4; Rev. ii.27, xi.1, xii.5, xix.15).[9]

But it is not enough simply to identify the two-handed engine as the rod of Christ the royal Judge of all mankind; the image in line 130 works more complexly. Coming as it does at the climax of a passage about bad pastors, "that two-handed engine" directs our thoughts to Christ's rod, the instrument of

divine justice, but also by so doing reminds us of the reference
we have heard ten lines earlier to "A Sheep-hook," a bishop's
crosier. For the pastoral authority symbolized by the crosier is
derived from the chief Shepherd, and the many Biblical sig-
nificances of rod and staff (Matt. xxv.32 among them) lie behind the complex symbolism which the Church developed for a
bishop's pastoral staff.

Daniel Rock's study of ritual and symbolism in the medieval English Church contains the following succinct description:

Wood, no doubt, though perhaps of the choicest kinds,
such as ebony, cedar, or cypress, furnished the material for the
pastoral staff in the earlier ages of the Church in this island; and
of wood, though (188) hidden by gilding, it is often made for the
Catholic bishops of this country to the present day. Churchmen
in the twelfth century purposely composed it from several materials: its stem was made of wood, shod with iron, blunted, not
sharp, at its foot, and surmounted by a small knob of rock-
crystal, or of one or another of the precious metals, from which
sprang out the crook itself, carved in ivory, with this sentence
running round it — *Dum iratus fueris, misericordiae recordaberis;* while upon the ball beneath was written the word *Homo,*
and the spike at the lower end bore this injunction — *Parce.*
Thus the bishop, by the very emblem of his high spiritual
power, was warned, though (189) angered, not to be wrathful —
to keep in remembrance, being but a man himself, he ought to
watch over his own heart, and let not the thoughts of his
dignity uplift him — and even while bringing the iron strength
and correction of Church-discipline to bear against sinners, still
he must be mild, not harsh.[10]

One of the earliest extant references comes from Isidore of
Seville, who implies that by his time the giving of the staff was
a familiar and long-established custom in the rite for the consecration of a bishop-elect.[11] The symbolism had been elaborately
developed by the twelfth century, when Honorius of Autun
wrote a detailed account of it in *Gemma Animae.* He traces its

34

origin back to Moses, who by God's command carried a rod
with which he performed deeds that terrified the enemies of
Israel, or fed God's flock, and with which he led them to a land
flowing with milk and honey. But Moses' rod was nothing other
than the pastoral staff, which some authors call *pedum* because
with its crook shepherds draw back the feet of wandering
sheep.[12] Honorius goes on to discuss how the pastoral staff symbolizes the delicate and difficult balance of governing, nourishing, rescuing, and punishing that a bishop has to maintain.[13]
Its materials of bone, wood, and crystal sphere signify respectively the hardness of the Law, the mildness of the Gospel, and
the divinity of Christ. The top suggests the kingdom of heaven,
but the hardness of iron at the lower end gives a fearful re-
minder that the time for preaching the gospel of eternal life
will come to an end in the Last Judgment.[14]

As Christ's rod may be considered the symbol and instrument of His royal authority, so the crosier (in one aspect of its
symbolism) is like a king's sceptre. Honorius says that "through
the rod, by which the wicked are purified, the power of rule is
figured." [15] Durandus concludes his chapter on the symbolism of
the staff by relating it to "that which agreeth unto the Head,
even Christ"; in this respect

the Bishop's Staff signifieth the power of Christ, whereof the
Psalmist saith, THE ROD OF THY KINGDOM IS A RIGHT
SCEPTRE, that is, a sceptre of direction, FOR THOU HAST
LOVED RIGHTEOUSNESS, AND HATED INIQUITY;
and elsewhere, THOU SHALT RULE THEM WITH A
ROD OF IRON. The hardness of the iron signifieth the might
of rightness, with which Christ SHALL BREAK THE UN-
RIGHTEOUS IN PIECES LIKE A POTTER'S VESSEL.
Yet is the power of Christ not the power of the rod alone,
but the power also of the Staff, for it doth not only chasten, but
sustaineth; whence the Psalmist, THY ROD AND THY
STAFF COMFORT ME.[16]

A comprehensive interpretation of "that two-handed engine" may now be summarily stated. Since the bad shepherds have not fed their flocks, the chief Shepherd (1 Pet. v.4) will smite them down with His rod, which is the archetypal reality behind every bishop's staff. Yet to say that the engine is Christ's rod, though strictly accurate if "is" means "denotes," seems inadequate to the full poetic force of the image. For it names one thing and simultaneously reminds us of another; such is the truly poetic function of this image, which has been so heavily freighted with meaning. It operates to remind us of "A Sheephook" (120) at the same time that it is pointing to the instrument of divine justice by which the sheep-hook will be abased, "that two-handed engine," the irresistible rod of Christ the divine Shepherd, King, and Judge. [17]

Milton has taken some pains to underscore, as a significant point for us to notice, the manner of holding the staff: "Blind mouthes! that scarce themselves know how to hold/A Sheephook" (119–120). Of the many different actions and attitudes that a bishop must be able to employ, rescue is the one being emphasized here; and the image totally reorganizes the feelings we have been carrying since line 75, with its image of a two-pronged instrument, "th' abhorred shears." Now, ten lines further on, our feelings are complexly reorganized again with the reference to Christ's two-handed engine at the Last Judgment. The bad shepherds will be among the goats, at the Judge's left hand. But the parable also mentions sheep at His right hand, so the image in the poem implies comfort for the righteous at the same time as it is explicitly threatening punishment for the wicked.

This interpretation accounts for "two-handed" as well as for "engine." If it is true, we may say that Milton is tapping a long tradition of ecclesiastical symbolism which was still current even in the Protestant England of his time,[18] and which had itself been derived from the Scriptures that he knew so intimately.

The Decorum of St. Peter's Speech

Two great pastoral sections of some length — John x.1–16 ("I am the good shepherd") and Ezekiel xxxiv ("Son of man, prophesy against the shepherds of Israel . . . that do feed themselves") — are certainly the main "sources" for lines 113–129 of St. Peter's speech. For lines 117–118 Milton also remembers the wedding feast of Matthew xxii and Luke xiv, which he transmutes into "the shearers feast" (decorum again).

Then, for the last two lines, which, for all the ferocity of their threat, are also to imply a suggestion of comfort and reassurance, he remembers Psalm xxiii and Isaiah x and all the other passages about rod and staff. Chiefly, though, he remembers Matthew xxv. By recalling that, and along with it — indeed by means of it — the centuries-old symbolism of the pastoral staff, he draws together a complex range of ideas and feelings. Doctrine and preaching (which the bad shepherds have neglected), excommunication and final judgment (which may be imminent), all come to mind. The young shepherd who sings for his dead friend may not be ready to perform the functions of his office; a greater Shepherd is. "Smite" comes, perhaps, from Isaiah x,[19] and the note of swift finality;[20] and these elements are blended with a suggestion from Ezekiel xxxiv.16: "I will seek that which was lost, and bring again that which was driven away, and will bind up that which was broken, and will strengthen that which was sick: but I will destroy the fat and the strong; I will feed them with judgment." St. Peter in *Lycidas*, like Ezekiel and like the first Evangelist, is bringing comfort to the righteous as he foretells punishment for the wicked, though certainly it is to the latter that he explicitly gives all his emphasis. For the Shepherd and Bishop of souls (1 Pet. ii.25) is at the door — indeed He is Himself the door (John x.7, 9); and He is ready to depose the hireling bishops in one swift, sure, terrible blow.

How, precisely, Milton does not know and does not say, although his alluding to Matthew xxv would indicate that thoughts of the Last Judgment are in his mind.[21] St. Peter's final couplet is meant, surely, to include an element of oracular mystery. By 1645, though, when Milton added the headnote, events had so vindicated his dark prophecy that he could say the author "by occasion foretells the ruine of our corrupted Clergie then in their height." No doubt the sentence gave him pleasure; *poeta vates est.*

The periphrasis that he devises for the climax of St. Peter's speech is the solution to a problem in the control of tone. Milton wants us to be aware of Christ's rod of justice, and at the same time, of its derivative, the pastoral staff which symbolizes the authority that the hireling bishops have abused. Obviously none of the words for the staff itself will do ("crook," "croche," "crose," "crosier," "staff," or the "Sheep-hook" of line 120). So he has to construct a very special form of words, one that will bring before our minds both Christ's rod and the crosier; and as usual he makes everything work for him. "That" functions as a simple demonstrative (as in "Not that faire field/Of Enna"); and perhaps also it is meant to help us recall "A Sheep-hook" from line 120. "Two-handed," besides pointing to Christ's rod in the parable of the Last Judgment, also magnifies, by its direct and obvious literal meaning, the sense of downward thrust which the image so powerfully conveys. And "engine" is exactly right for the note of menace. All in all, one may feel that Milton has solved the artistic problem with great dexterity; the principle of its solution is decorum, that grand masterpiece.[22]

II

Of the several lines of argument that may be anticipated against the interpretation here proposed, we may first consider one arising from the subordinate implication I have claimed for the image in line 130. If the two-handed engine is Christ's rod of justice which will be brought to bear against bishops who neglect the responsibility symbolized by the crosier, one may ask what ideas, if any, Milton and his original audience had about that item of episcopal insignia. For ever since 1552 all mention of the crosier had been omitted from the Anglican Ordinal and from every other part of the Prayer Book. Did the use of it, did even the knowledge of its symbolism, survive into Milton's time?

Use of the staff was expressly directed in the first Prayer Book (1549),[23] and in the first Anglican Ordinal (1550) the order for the consecration of a bishop-elect rubrically prescribed that a staff should be delivered into the hand of the new bishop as the consecrator spoke the prescribed formula.[24] The second Ordinal (which was authorized as part of the 1552 Prayer Book), while saying nothing either to direct or to prohibit use of the staff, omitted the 1550 rubric but retained the formula, conflated now with that for the delivery of the Bible;[25] and the Elizabethan Prayer Book of 1559 did the same. The question therefore arises, What was the practice in the Elizabethan, Jacobean, and Caroline church with respect to the pastoral staff? It is a complicated question, of course, which has been much studied; and the answer to it will obviously affect the validity of a part of the interpretation I have offered for St. Peter's speech in *Lycidas*. The authoritative discussion of the problem in our century, the Report written by five Anglican bishops and published in 1908 by the Convocation of Canterbury, concludes that "whatever may be the meaning of the phrase 'episcopalibus insigniis decoravit' in the Registers, there can, we think, be no doubt that a pastoral staff or crosier is a legal ornament of a Bishop in the Church of England . . . It fell indeed rapidly into general disuse . . . but it was never, in any sense, abolished, and it has been revived (with general approval or acquiescence) in the generation immediately preceding our own." [26]

Evidence that the idea of the pastoral staff remained current into Milton's time and beyond survives in three forms:

(1) According to the *Canterbury Report* (p. 103), Bishop Wren's staff, "the only extant seventeenth-century staff certainly designed for actual use," is preserved with his mitre at Pembroke College, Cambridge. Another, "which was found in an attic in St. John's College, Oxford . . . and which is now preserved in a glass case in the library, may *possibly* have belonged to Archbishop Laud . . . It seems almost too good to have been a merely funeral ornament used, as some suppose, at the elaborate obsequies of Archbishop Juxon."

(2) Pastoral staves are represented on a number of brass and marble effigies of post-Reformation bishops; an exhaustive list appears in Appendix B of the *Canterbury Report* (pp. 110–120). Note also the mention (p. 103) of "the curious alabaster effigy of Walter de Merton, +1277, in Rochester Cathedral, erected in 1598 at the instance of the Warden of Merton College, Sir H. Saville. It represents the Bishop partly in the dress of the sixteenth century, and with a staff the head or crook of which resembles the modern shepherd's crook."

Several brasses are pictured in H. J. Clayton's *The Ornaments of the Ministers as Shown on English Monumental Brasses:*[27] Thomas Goodryke, or Goodrich, Bishop of Ely, d. 1554 (p. 34); Henry Robinson, Bishop of Carlisle and Provost of Queen's College, Oxford, d. 1616 (p. 40); and, most interesting of all for us as being nearest in date to *Lycidas*, Samuel Harsnett, Archbishop of York, d. 1631 (p. 22). The latter is pictured also in *Hierurgia Anglicana*.[28]

(3) A mass of documentary evidence for "Mitres, Pastoral Staffs, and Processional Crosses" in the period 1546–1785 appears in *Hierurgia Anglicana*, Part I, pp. 223–235.[29]

It is clear that knowledge of the crosier and its symbolism certainly remained current into Milton's time, and that possibly the ritual use of it was continued here and there. To that extent my interpretation of *Lycidas* 130 is safe. It is still necessary, however, to meet an allied objection that was expressed by a friend who did me the favor of reading an earlier version of this essay, and was not persuaded.

Milton, he believes, simply would not use in this way an item from the episcopal insignia. It may be said in reply that the poet we all think of as Puritan has already admitted into his poem references to *two* such items, to the mitre in line 112 explicitly,[30] and figuratively to the crosier in line 120. To meet my friend's criticism we must ask how relevant Milton's Puritan sympathies are for an understanding of the image in lines 130–131 and more generally for the whole passage, lines 108–131.

Obviously Milton is presenting St. Peter as a leader of the clergy, in some sense; and at least one reason why he can accept for the purpose the familiar symbolism of the mitre is that it brings together a rich concentration of Biblical ideas. The staff carries rich meanings too, equally Biblical. Whatever in 1637 Milton's thought may have been concerning the proper administration of church discipline, he is clearly using the staff to symbolize pastoral responsibilities; he can do so consistently with belief that the fullness of pastoral responsibility belongs either to all, or only to some chief members, of the ordained clergy. On either assumption, the traditional symbolism of the staff is peculiarly apt for focusing the criticism he wants to voice against the unsatisfactory men who now hold authority in the Church of England as its chief pastors and who will be brought to account under the authority of the Chief Shepherd Himself. The interpretation I have offered for the two-handed engine is thus not affected by our ability or inability to define with full precision all the details of Milton's opinion about episcopacy because lines 108–131 are consistent with any theory of episcopacy that he could have held. I shall argue that his thought in the passage involves a necessary reference to only one single item among the several items that would or could have been included in his full thought about the meaning of "bishop," but that he does point up his sense of outrage over the inconsistency between what Anglican formularies officially endorse and what Anglican bishops of the time are actually doing (or rather, as Milton would say, leaving undone).

We really do not know what his opinions on church government were at this period. The passage involving St. Peter shows that by this date he certainly believed England to be afflicted with bad bishops; it is not clear that he had already decided that episcopacy itself was bad.[31] He never found it necessary to cancel "Miter'd" and "Sheep-hook," even when to our certain knowledge he had decided that prelatical episcopacy ought to be rooted out. Suppose we did know, however, that he had already reached by 1637 the position we know he had reached by the early 1640's. What would follow?

His known opposition to prelatical episcopacy in the 1640's has helped to persuade some interpreters that the passage in *Lycidas* against the hireling shepherds is best illuminated by reference to ideas from English and continental Protestant reformers (as distinguished from Anglican supporters of episcopacy), reformers speaking from a tradition hostile to episcopacy as such and also distinguished by emphasis on preaching as supreme among the gifts by which the Church is divinely empowered to fulfill her mission in the world.[32] Certainly the passage reflects intense dissatisfaction with the quality of preaching, and the attitude toward it, in the English Church of 1637. We do not have to seek in the Puritan tradition, however, for an explanation of Milton's assumptions. His thought is based much closer to home, and the result is a far more telling thrust against the bishops' carelessness about preaching than anything he could have produced from exclusively Puritan assumptions.

The Decorum of St. Peter's Speech

If by 1637 Milton has arrived at root-and-branch opposition to episcopacy, the logic of his stance in lines 108–131 vis-à-vis the prelatical Church of England may be spelled out somewhat as follows: "My point is that bishops should preach — whatever bishops are. I could indeed show what the New Testament concept of ἐπίσκοπος includes and does not include, but that is unnecessary just now. One idea alone is relevant here: I do certainly hold that every bishop is meant to be a preacher of the Word. So do you, as your own formularies make abundantly clear. How, then, can you condone your bishops' carelessness toward the high responsibility that you yourself enjoin upon each one at his consecration?" So Milton could say even if he were writing his poem out of root-and-branch opposition to episcopacy, and he could still be employing the symbolism I have claimed for his references to episcopal mitre and staff. And if (as I think far more likely) his position was not yet so extreme, his tone might be less strident but his point and his symbolism would remain just the same. "Bishops ought to be preachers. You are allowing our bishops to neglect their responsibility, and yet at every consecration you declare your belief in a preaching episcopate."

Besides requiring that certain questions be put to the bishop-elect about his determination to instruct, teach, and exhort the people out of the Holy Scriptures, "The Fourme of Consecrating of an Archebisshoppe, or Bisshoppe" makes quite explicit the Church's expectation that her bishops are meant to be preachers. The final prayer before the benediction is based on a prayer from a medieval form (in the Sarum Pontifical) for the Enthronement of a Bishop; and the Latin prayer itself is based on several verses in the Pastoral Epistles (2 Tim. iv.2; 1 Tim. iv.12; 2 Tim. iv.7–8):

Most merciful father, we beseche thee to send down vpon this thy seruant, thy heauenly blessynge, and so endue hym with thy holy spirite, that he preaching thy worde, may not only be earneste to reproue, beseche, and rebuke with al pacience and doctryne, but also may be to such as beleue, an wholesome example, in worde, in conuersacion, in loue, in faith, in chastitie, and puritie, that faythfully fulfilling his course, at the latter day he maye receiue the croune of righteousnesse, laied vp by the Lord, the righteous iudge, who liueth, and reigneth, one god with the father and *the* holy gost, worlde withoute ende. Amen.[33]

Even more revealing for our purpose of interpreting the image of the two-handed engine is the Anglican formula for the delivery of the Bible to a newly consecrated bishop, a formula that dates from 1552. Milton would not be likely to overlook the fact that it conflates what in 1550 had been two distinct formulas for two separate actions, the laying of the Bible upon the neck of the newly consecrated bishop (now in 1552 the delivery of the Bible into his hands), and the delivery of the crosier; and almost certainly he would register the effect of the conflation.

Geue hede vnto reading, exhortacion and doctrine. Thinke vpon these thinges conteined in this boke, be diligent in them, that the encrease comyng therby, may be manyfest vnto all men. Take hede vnto thy selfe, and vnto teaching, and be diligent in doing them, for by doing this, thou shalt saue thy selfe, and them that heare thee:[34] be to the flocke of Christ a shepeheard, not a wolfe: feede them, deuoure them not: holde vp the weake, heale the sicke, binde together the broken, bryng againe the outcastes, seke the lost. Be so mercifull, that you be not to remisse, so minister discipline, that *you* forgeat not mercy: that whē the chief shepheard shal come, ye may receyue the immarcessible croune of glory, through Iesus Christ our lord. *Amen.*[35]

With a few minor changes in diction (such as "appear" for "come" and "never-fading" for "immarcessible"), this formula has been used for the delivery of the Bible in every Anglican consecration since 1552. In it the study and preaching of the Bible are clearly being viewed as specifically *pastoral* responsibilities of a bishop. Could anything be closer to the assumptions behind St. Peter's speech in *Lycidas*?

But, of course, some among those who argue that the two-handed engine is the sword of God's justice have been reminding us all along that the Bible, the Word of God, is the sword of the Spirit. We may turn now to consider the argument for the sword, which in recent years has been developed with much learning and skill.[36] Indeed, de Beer has written that "until it is definitely disproved the sword has a strong claim to be the particular weapon to which Milton refers." [37] In strict logic no interpretation, probably, can be either proved or disproved, but several points may be noted that tend to weaken the argument for the sword.

(1) Probably one reason why the sword has so often commended itself to interpreters is that Scriptural authority can be found for a "two-edged" sword (Ps. cxlix.6; Heb. iv.12; Rev. i.16, ii.12). All arguments based on such texts, however, fail to suggest any reason why Milton should have changed "two-edged" to "two-handed."

(2) One of the Biblical texts cited by both de Beer and Le Comte is Zech. xiii.7: "Awake, O sword, against my shepherd, and against the man that is my fellow, saith the Lord of hosts: smite the shepherd, and the sheep shall be scattered: and I will turn mine hand upon the little ones." Here, though, it is a good shepherd who is being spoken of, the Lord's "fellow" (as de Beer notes, p. 62), and therefore Jesus can use the verse about Himself (Matt. xxvi.31; Mk. xiv.27). This text, then, is irrelevant.

(3) Another text is Zech. xi.17, which does indeed associate bad shepherds and punishment by the sword: "Woe to the idol

shepherd that leaveth the flock! the sword shall be upon his arm, and upon his right eye: his arm shall be clean dried up, and his right eye shall be utterly darkened." By itself, however, this one verse constitutes very slight reason for deciding that the two-handed engine is a sword rather than Christ's rod, for which numerous Biblical texts can be relevantly cited.

(4) The other Biblical texts that have been used in various arguments for the sword do not associate sword and shepherds. The texts can be divided into four categories:

(a) Four of them make no explicit mention of a sword: Jer. l.25; 2 Thess. ii.8; Rev. xix.11, 13.

(b) Four do not represent the sword as an instrument of punishment: Isa. xlix.2; Matt. x.34; Heb. iv.12; Rev. i.16.

(c) Of those that do mention the sword as an instrument of warfare against evildoers, or punishment of them, all but one speak of the wicked generally (Deut. xxviii.22; Ps. cxlix. 5–9; Rev. xix.15) or of such general groups as the Philistines (Jer. xlvii.6) or unfaithful Israel (Ezek. xxi) or imperfect Christians at Pergamos (Rev. ii.12–16). Whereas, if "that two-handed engine" means the rod of Christ (which is a *pastoral* instrument, as well as a royal and judicial one), the application can be limited to bad bishops — appropriately, since St. Peter's speech has been focused, throughout, upon the hireling shepherds.[38]

(d) The one exception mentioned in (c) above is Eph. vi.17 (". . . the sword of the Spirit, which is the word of God"), against the relevance of which a rather special case can be made. It is the last item in a passage about the armor of a Christian (vv. 11–17), and the introduction to the passage shows precisely who the enemies a Christian must fight against are understood to be (vv. 11–12). The enemies are not human beings at all, but supernatural powers of evil, "the rulers of the darkness of this world." Therefore, no valid argument can be drawn from Eph. vi.17 for interpreting St. Peter's speech in

46

Lycidas, where the persons being denounced are simply human and — quite specifically — bad shepherds.

Such is the case that I would offer against the sword as the reference in line 130. But sword and rod derive equally from the Bible. The question therefore arises, What positive arguments can be adduced to suggest that Christ's rod is the more probable reference? Two lines of evidence suggest themselves.

(1) If the first line of *Lycidas* alludes to Hebrews xii.26,[39] lines 130–131 of the poem, by echoing line 1, will again remind us of the passage in Hebrews. The New English Bible, alone among translations I have seen, gives to a key phrase in verse 27 (which I have italicized in the quotation below) an emphasis that may remind us of "smite once, and smite no more"; it will be helpful to have the whole context before us, in that version:

Remember where you stand: not before the palpable, blazing fire of Sinai, with the darkness, gloom, and whirlwind, the trumpet-blast and the oracular voice, which they heard, and begged to hear no more. . . .
No, you stand before Mount Zion and the city of the living God, heavenly Jerusalem, before myriads of angels, the full concourse and assembly of the first-born citizens of heaven, and God the judge of all, and the spirits of good men made perfect, and Jesus the mediator of a new covenant, whose sprinkled blood has better things to tell than the blood of Abel. See that you do not refuse to hear the voice that speaks. Those who refused to hear the oracle speaking on earth found no escape; still less shall we escape if we refuse to hear the One who speaks from heaven. Then indeed his voice shook the earth, but now he has promised, 'Yet once again I will shake not earth alone, but the heavens also.'[40] The words 'once again' — *and only once* — imply that the shaking of these created things means their removal, and then what is not shaken will remain. The kingdom we are given is unshakable; let us therefore give thanks to God, and so worship him as he would be worshipped, with reverence and awe; for our God is a devouring fire. (Hebrews xii.18–29)

The contrast in this passage between the transitory and the enduring, with its promise to the faithful of a heavenly consummation for all temporal experience, sounds an apocalyptic note that involves, perhaps, a reference to the Second Coming and the Last Judgment. If so, an echo of Hebrews xii.26 in *Lycidas* 130–131 would tend to confirm that *Lycidas* 130 is alluding to Matthew xxv.32, which in turn would confirm the pastoral character of "that two-handed engine" through the suggestion of a shepherd's rod in Matthew xxv.32.[41]

(2) A more extended chain of evidence may be found in the pattern of imagery that begins with the introduction of St. Peter. "Miter'd" signals the arrival, in the procession of mourners, of a chief pastor in the Church. Then we hear "young swain," "the fold," "the shearers feast," "A Sheep-hook," "the faithfull Herdmans art," "songs," "scrannel Pipes," "The hungry Sheep," "the grim Woolf" — a succession that carries us from line 112 to line 128. With unfailing consistency the whole passage has been laced with pastoral imagery; and "the shearers feast" is, for so faithful a Biblicist as Milton, a notably bold transmutation of Scripture.[42] Surely we are being led to anticipate that the pastoral vein will be kept up straight through to the end of the passage, and a reference to Christ's rod in the image of the two-handed engine would mean that pastoral imagery is indeed being sustained without interruption.[43]

III

From the thesis of this essay it follows that understanding of *Lycidas* has occasionally been blurred, and therefore appreciation of Milton's art in general has been proportionately weakened, because we have assumed that he is willing to break his pastoral mold. The assumption arises because we overlook the consistency with which he follows decorum, and because we mistake the meaning of certain lines. "That strain I heard was of a higher mood" (87) does acknowledge the presence of something above the pastoral — but in a passage (78–84) that is introduced by a deliberate recollection (77) of Virgil's pastoral world (Eclogue VI, 3–4). And, to be prosily literal, the other place — "Return *Alpheus*, the dread voice is past,/That shrunk thy streams" (132–133) — does not say that the dread voice destroyed the streams. The willingness to suppose that these lines acknowledge moments when the pastoral mode is totally suppressed, or even destroyed, is of a piece with the willingness to believe in that old mirage, "the digressions in *Lycidas*." In the former age we had been conditioned to approach the poem expecting that kind of behavior (though from the greatest classical artist in English), and so of course we seemed to find it. We have got over the delusion, but we still approach the poem assuming that at any moment Milton may throw away his pastoral conventions: in Phoebus' lines, in St. Peter's speech as a whole, in the image of the two-handed engine — anywhere he pleases.

He is not that kind of poet. He will use one *genre* after another, and he will adapt and push and strain to the limit. He will transform every mold he touches, completely. But he will not break it.

A Poem about Loss

I

Paradise is not lost, in Milton's great epic, until the last paragraph of the last book. Although the irreversible, catastrophic acts of choice are made back in Book IX, it is the expulsion from the Garden that consummates the loss; and that does not occur until the very end. What happens between those two widely separated points is a sequence of events that transform the way Adam feels, and the way readers feel, about the whole idea of loss. We do not have to fear that we have moved beyond all the best things in the poem when we have finished reading about the temptation and fall.

After the destructive choices have been made in Book IX, the mind of Adam and Eve, their moral consciousness, becomes the chief *locus* for the dramatic action, which, having taken this turn inward, continues without interruption straight through to the last words of the poem. At the conclusion of Book IX, Adam and Eve are frail and familiar humanity fallen away from grace and therefore totally incapacitated to escape from their predicament by their own resources. The brief judgment scene early in Book X (92–223) is quiet, laconic almost, intimate and domestic. The final section of the same book (beginning with Adam's soliloquy at 720ff.), though much longer, uses a similarly intimate perspective, with a great intensification of the participants' emotions, viewed from very close. By the end of Book X, harmony between Adam and Eve has been restored; and though they themselves do not yet know it, they have taken their first step toward restoration to the life of grace. After they both receive from Michael the news of their sentence to expulsion, early in Book XI, Adam watches with profound emotional involvement the series of visions that comes to its climax with the awesome revelation of the flood and its astonishing sequel the rainbow. Then in the final book his experience in the narrative revelation leads to his spiritual regeneration through his act of accepting God's offer of inward renewal, and Eve proceeds to a

53

similar act of will in response to the same revelation given to her in a dream.

Thus, the three last books are occupied with narrating a complicated process of moral and spiritual action that goes on within the consciousness of the two main characters.[1] Such an action, if adequately managed by a poet, will necessarily involve the most elaborate interweaving of psychological and theological subtleties. The purpose of this essay is to trace several closely related themes that stand out prominently in the action as it moves in this inward manner to its conclusion.

The first instance of what is going to be the pattern of Adam's dramatic experience in the last two books occurs early in Book XI even before Michael arrives. Adam has learned something that causes him to change his mind. Prayer works (141–155), and from that advance in true knowledge he makes a false inference: "the bitterness of death/Is past, and we shall live" (157–158). A new insight, from which he moves to a false conclusion, which then has to be corrected, which in turn starts the sequence over again: such is the detailed local pattern of Adam's experience from now on, which develops by means of a relationship with Michael that is genuinely dramatic, dynamic, shifting from moment to moment. He comments. He asks questions. He lets his emotions, his sympathies and hopes, be strongly engaged. He makes moral judgments. He makes decisions, performs acts of will.

Michael's role as an agent in the drama grows more personal in Book XII. Earlier he has served as the interpreter of vision, more or less detached. In the last book, partly because it is his own speech that must mediate the revelation, he is drawn into greater dramatic involvement with Adam. Occasionally he allows himself a direct expression of his emotions (105–106, 115–120, 537–539). In his treatment of geographical details (128–146, 156–159) and by certain other touches (116,

128, 342) he manifests some sense of intimacy. But mainly he urges, repeatedly and with some sternness, that Adam recognize his personal responsibility for the disaster (79–84, 285–286, 386–392).

Through his relationship with Michael, Adam experiences an inward drama of moral consciousness that carries to its resolution the action in which he has been directly involved since Book IV. His feelings about loss, and ours, are transformed by that dramatic experience. Indeed the entire poem, the long stretch of its total length, is needed to effect a development in idea and emotion that comes about chiefly through a transformation in the meaning of three key words: "loss," "death," and "wrath." This organic development proceeds continuously at all the levels (action, character, thought, diction); and the result by the time we have finished Book XII is an extraordinary complication in thought and feeling, both for the two central characters in the story and for us, the readers of the poem.

II

The development in the theme of loss comes about largely through a transformation in the idea of death. Adam enters the poem with no clear notion of what death may be, except that it is "Som dreadful thing no doubt" (IV.426) and that his Maker takes it very seriously indeed (VIII.333–337). We know what it is because we have already seen an elaborate image of it: a place and a mode of existence, even a kind of living, in which personality continues to act, but in endless pain and frustration. Death is, of course, the loss of life, and Hell is its country, a world of lost persons who have lost a war, lost happiness, lost Heaven, yet keep insisting they have not lost everything.

The first two books of *Paradise Lost* offer a variety of perspectives on the idea. Satan grimly makes allowance for still more loss to come in Hell (I.269–270), and Moloch is willing to entertain even the prospect of annihilation (II.47–49, 95–98). Belial is not, "for who would loose,/Though full of pain, this intellectual being . . . ?" (II.146–147). In the council at Pandaemonium the theme moves from Satan's "I give not Heav'n for lost" (II.14), through the narrator's "A fairer person lost not Heav'n" (110 — an ambiguous arrangement of words that can be thought in both directions), to Beelzebub's frank acknowledgment of "loss/Irreparable" (330–331). Then while he and Satan are feeling hugely satisfied at their efficient winding up of the debate, the narrator renews the true perspective with two poignant glimpses of intellectual and spiritual loss: the philosophic devils can find "no end, in wandring mazes lost" (561), and all the devils pine for "one small drop" of Lethe, "to loose/ In sweet forgetfulness all pain and woe" (607–608). In fact all these persons are dead, "dead in sins and lost" as man is going to be (III.233). It is appalling even to think of. For something contradictory and unnatural has occurred if immortal spirits suffer change and loss; and one of the most important things we are being shown in the opening scenes is the monstrousness of death,[2] as finally becomes explicit for us in that terrible passage of Book II where image and paradox and tremendous energy of sound bring to its climax the long representation of Hell (618–628).

And then before long we are shown that the true monarch in this realm of death is not Satan, that incestuous usurper, but a shapeless monster black as night, who, though Satan's son, is Satan's king. Death has by now become a person, in the characterization of whom details of imagery and action gradually bring out the appropriate suggestions of bodily death.[3] There are also hints of a power for total destruction. He brandishes a "mortal Dart" (II.729), "Made to destroy" (II.787); "that mortal dint,/Save he who reigns above, none can resist" (II.813–814).

Thus by the end of Book II the word "death" has been made so polysemantic that it can serve thenceforth as one of the most complexly evocative of all the words in the special vocabulary of the poem. Milton will be using it to signify either a character in the story; or a mode of penal existence characterized by loss and eternal misery, pain, and frustration; or — as Adam and Eve imagine will be their fate — an event or experience that simply ends existence by an act of final destruction.

Milton dramatizes the interplay of the latter two meanings in Adam's long soliloquy after the judgment scene. Dust, dust, dust, though the prospect leaves him horrified as it keeps recurring (X.748, 770, 805), yet seems preferable to endless woe. His agonized meditation leads him to the much worse conception of his own immortality (782–789) and of "deathless Death" (798), "endless miserie" (810); "both Death and I/Am found Eternal" (815–816). Thus he discovers perpetual existence in loss and pain; what had given, so to speak, some comfort to the devils, what had furnished the starting-point for so much of the debate and so much of the "hope" in Hell, seems to Adam the worst fate of all. So death's delay makes him complain (771–782), and complain again (850ff.). For in the long run, what "death" really signifies to Adam and Eve after their sin is extinction. Although the mild Judge has deferred the "Immediate dissolution" (X.1049) that they had been expecting, nevertheless an earthly existence indefinite in duration but doomed at last to certain extinction is what they anticipate — "till we end/In dust, our final rest and native home" (X.1084–1085).[4]

This is the meaning of "death" that will dominate the rest of the poem. Whatever it is, whether translation into an endless existence of woe or the simpler horror of annihilation, death is an intolerable loss. Only, Adam and Eve do not know that there can be something else, too, something that, while leaving intact the deadly seriousness of their doom, will lift them right out of its grasp. The something else is divine rescue. They know God as creator, lord, all-giver;[5] they have never conceived or imagined that He might also be redeemer. By elaborating the theme of redemption — the amazing, the totally unexpected and unmerited, divine act of rescue — Milton transforms our idea of loss and the entire structure of feelings that we associate with it.

The transformation results from a radical change of perspective, which is not fully accomplished until the end of the poem but which Milton, characteristically, starts to effect very promptly, as soon as he has succeeded in communicating (by the speeches of Book X) Adam and Eve's notion of death. At the beginning of Book XI the Son speaks of bodily death as the way to redeemed life (40–44), and the Father sees it as a blessing. Man having lost the gift of happiness, the other gift of immortality would only have served

> . . . to eternize woe;
> Till I provided Death; so Death becomes
> His final remedie . . .
> (XI.60–62)[6]

Indeed the preparation for this change of perspective on death and loss has been made long before, with the first scene in Heaven. Hell's egocentricity expresses itself in hate (a word that occurs, with its cognates, twelve times in the first two books) and results in the loss of integrity of body, mind, and soul (IV.846–850, 904–911); in the end the devils lose control of even their shape.[7] With the opening scene in Heaven we begin to develop a positive sense of what they have lost: life, or more suggestively, Life, the world of love, whose characteristic action is to give. With typical indirectness Milton has begun

that theme in Satan's "I give not Heav'n for lost" (II.14).[8] One
continuous and developing action of divine giving constitutes
the movement of the first scene in Book III, which — also
typically — begins to complicate the theme of loss. First the
angels receive "Beatitude past utterance" from the vision of God
(62). The Father next declares His will that man, who "had
of mee/All he could have" (97–98), though by sin "loosing all"
(206), yet "shall find grace" (131), "grace in me/Freely voutsaft" (174–175).[9] Then the Son, who has received life by gift
from the Father (243–244), offers to give that life for man's
redemption. Last the Father, in the great final speech, brings all
the themes together and confers still another, supreme, gift upon
the Son:

> . . . *well thou know'st how dear,*
> *To me are all my works, nor Man the least*
> *Though last created, that for him I spare*
> *Thee from my bosom and right hand, to save,*
> *By loosing thee a while, the whole Race lost.*
>
> . . . .
>
> *So Heav'nly love shall outdoo Hellish hate*
> *Giving to death, and dying to redeeme,*
>
> . . . .
>
> *Here shalt thou sit incarnate, here shalt Reign*
> *Both God and Man, Son both of God and Man,*
> *Anointed universal King, all Power*
> *I give thee, reign for ever, and assume*
> *Thy Merits . . .*
>   (III.276–319)

But of course Adam does not learn about all this until he
receives the revelation from Michael. Until almost the very last
moment of the poem, indeed, he continues to assume that ultimately his fate is going to be dissolution, extinction. We know
better, and our ironic perspective is one of Milton's chief ways of

making the scene dramatically exciting for us. We keep waiting for the moment when Adam will grasp the point that he need not end in dust.

It is a long time coming. The visions of Book XI have had as their purpose the revelation to Adam of the meaning of death, physical death chiefly. Then as he listens to Michael's narratives in Book XII, he is concentrating mainly on "The Womans seed," who he will be and how he will bruise the Serpent's head.[10] The successive stages of the narrative, which gradually answer the questions for him, lead him forward through a series of more and more excited responses, from the relatively calm speech, "O sent from Heav'n,/Enlightner of my darkness" (XII. 270ff.), through the stronger feelings of the next, "O Prophet of glad tidings, finisher/Of utmost hope!" (375ff.), on to his ecstatic outburst on *felix culpa*, "O goodness infinite, goodness immense!" (469ff.) Even the latter, however, could not serve the purposes of the story Milton is telling if it were Adam's final word, because up to this point he still has given no evidence of understanding that he need not end in dust. Both before and during the visions of Book XI he has consistently failed to pick up several hints from Michael that death may not, after all, finally terminate each human existence (365–366, 457–459, 469–470, 709–710); and all the time he is receiving the long narrative of how his dreadful loss will be avenged, he is not forgetting that death still awaits him personally, and that it means (as he believes) extinction. From the narratives of Book XII, indeed, it is clear to him that all men are going to die (434–435, 444–445). Not until the conclusion of Michael's last narrative does Adam perceive how men may nevertheless still triumph over death — through resurrection, in which all may share who will accept the gift of salvation through the Son (539–546).

To that revelation he does respond in the way we have

been expecting. Rhetorically his final speech, very slow at first
as he tries to realize the wonders he has seen and heard, then
gradually smoothing out into the consummate poise of the third
and final sentence, leads straight to the line we have waited so
long to hear, and after that, on to the explicit confession of
faith:

> *Henceforth I learne . . .*
>
> . . . .
>
> *. . . that suffering for Truths sake*
> *Is fortitude to highest victorie,*
> *And to the faithful Death the Gate of Life;*
> *Taught this by his example whom I now*
> *Acknowledge my Redeemer ever blest.*
> (XII.561–573)

Immediately after this speech the gradually intensifying waves
of joy and wonder which have composed the dominant emotional pattern of Book XII and by which our whole feeling
about loss has been transformed come to their glowing climax in
the marvelous sentence that opens Michael's last speech:

> *This having learnt, thou hast attaind the summe*
> *Of wisdome; hope no higher, though all the Starrs*
> *Thou knewst by name, and all th' ethereal Powers,*
> *All secrets of the deep, all Natures works,*
> *Or works of God in Heav'n, Aire, Earth, or Sea,*
> *And all the riches of this World enjoydst,*
> *And all the rule, one Empire; onely add*
> *Deeds to thy knowledge answerable, add Faith,*
> *Add vertue, Patience, Temperance, add Love,*
> *By name to come call'd Charitie, the soul*
> *Of all the rest: then wilt thou not be loath*
> *To leave this Paradise, but shalt possess*
> *A paradise within thee, happier farr.*
> (XII.575–587)[11]

By means of this long-extended process Milton enormously complicates the structure of feelings that we associate with the idea of loss. For although we have been seeing Adam "Replete with joy and wonder" (468) through much of Book XII, a very different order of emotions has also been present simultaneously. The sinfulness of men against which supernal grace contends has figured very prominently in the narratives. All of it has come into the world because of Adam, and with some sternness Michael has repeatedly urged him to face his own personal responsibility for the disaster (XII.79–84, 285–286, 386–392). Now, as in his final speech Adam sums up what he has learned, we sense an austere discipline undergirding the ardent joy he is mastering. Michael's glorious sentence too, for all its incandescence, reduces most of its splendors into a concessive clause, and thus acts to sober in the same moment it celebrates them. A very conspicuous toning down occurs through the rest of his speech. Its end makes quite explicit, indeed physically exhibits, the complementary notes on which the poem is moving to its close: guilt that will always be remembered though confessed and absolved, and a sense of loss that will endure through all time, at the very center of a sober joy in the promise:

> *That ye may live, which will be many dayes,*
> *Both in one Faith unanimous though sad,*
> *With cause for evils past, yet much more cheer'd*
> *With meditation on the happie end.*
> (XII.602–605)

The lines describe the precise shape of human loss as we have by this late moment in the poem been led to understand it. Loss remains loss, but it is encompassed by the divine mercy. Or to state the point another way, an enduring sense of loss, being permeated by the operation of divine mercy, is transmuted into a different kind of "loss."

Now we are ready for the subtle complexities of emotion

in the lovely speech from Eve that ends the dialogue. Her very last words enact with the most delicate sensitivity a harmonious blending of the many varied feelings with which the two main characters will depart from the Garden:

> . . . *though all by mee is lost,*
> *Such favour I unworthie am voutsaft,*
> *By mee the Promis'd Seed shall all restore.*
> (XII.621–623)

It is a confession entirely open, full of shame, yet totally un-abashed, mixing humility and amazement and acceptance. On that complex note this poem about loss will end.

Some readers have felt, however, that because of its poig-nance the conclusion of the poem does not convincingly follow from the predominantly joyous body of Book XII.[12] A reply to that judgment may be developed from a consideration of "wrath," the third among the key words mentioned above whose meaning is transformed in the course of the poem. With the introduction of this word we approach the question of Milton's attitude toward his theme. He assesses it as supremely heroic, more so than that of any of his predecessors among the epic poets, an

> . . . *argument*
> *Not less but more Heroic then the wrauth*
> *Of stern* Achilles *on his Foe pursu'd*
> *Thrice Fugitive about* Troy Wall; *or rage*
> *Of* Turnus *for* Lavinia *disespous'd,*
> *Or* Neptun's *ire or* Juno's, *that so long*
> *Perplex'd the* Greek *and* Cytherea's Son . . .
> (IX.13–19)

As Todd explained, elaborating on remarks by some of his predecessors, Milton makes this claim because his theme is the wrath of the one true God:

His theme was more sublime than the wrath of Achilles, celebrated by Homer in the *Iliad;* of Turnus, by Virgil in the
Aeneid; or of Neptune, by Homer in the *Odyssey:* It therefore
demanded the invocation of *answerable style* to describe it. And,
as Mr. Richardson observes, though several other particulars are
specified as parts of his present subject, v. 6, &.; that of *the
anger of God,* v. 10, was the consequence of those, and is his
only subject. It is this which he places in opposition *to the anger
of men and gods:* in which, as Dr. Newton remarks, he has the
advantage of Homer and Virgil; the anger of the true God being
an "argument not less but *more* heroick." [13]

Like "loss" and "death," the phrase "wrath of God" means
at the end of the poem something different from what it means
at the beginning. By the end of Book XII we have been led to
feel how strange, complex, unpredictable a thing it is, the wrath
of God. Toward the rebellious angels, who "by thir own suggestion fell,/Self-tempted, self-deprav'd" (III.129–130), it is anger and unremitting hostility. Toward man too, after his foul
distrust, disloyalty, revolt, and disobedience (IX.6–7), the posture of Heaven, "Now alienated," is "distance and distaste,/
Anger and just rebuke, and judgement giv'n" (IX.9–10). But
also, redemptive grace is given to man. What is fresh and new
about the treatment Milton works out for this familiar idea is
the wonderful capaciousness he achieves in idea and tone by
developing his theme of a divine wrath that, while remaining
wrath, is something else too.

The general theme of wrath — the Father's and other characters' — has been growing from the first scene of the poem. Of
the important words that carry it ("anger," "appease," "avenge,"
"fury," "ire," "rage," "revenge," "wrath"), "rage" and "revenge"
dominate the opening, especially Book II. "Anger" and "wrath"
and the much less frequent "ire," apparently interchangeable,
are all ascribed by good characters, without embarrassment, to

the Father; Milton is hardly the man to underplay that great
Biblical theme, the wrath of God.

And yet he does underplay it, for he never tires of re-
joicing that rebellious men are not in God's eyes the enemies
that rebellious angels are (e.g., III.399–400; cf. II. 368–369); to
make the point inescapably clear is one of the purposes of the
Father's opening speech (III.80–134). By that stage in the
narrative we have had two books of furious anger and hate from
characters who see God's wrath as rage (I.95; II.144). Now that
the Father has a chance to speak for Himself (in a speech that
with some cause almost everybody regrets, to be sure), we hear
the reason for the divine wrath expounded at length, yet without one single occurrence of the words "wrath" and "anger."
Sound is very important. Perhaps if we hear the sound structure
truly, we may sense the Father's mildness, surely the effect His
speech is meant to produce, however the intention may have
been fumbled; we are meant to hear, while remembering all the
rage of I and II, a serene and imperturbable divine voice.[14]
The scene as a whole operates to encourage the impression of a
terrible wrath that no creature can endure, and yet to disengage
from that impression every hint of petulance and passion.[15] It
is a wrath which the sacrifice by the Son will cause to "be no
more" (264); after the resurrection the Son will return to
Heaven "to see thy face, wherein no cloud/Of anger shall remain, but peace assur'd,/And reconcilement" (262–264). Man
"shall find grace" (131), because the Father wills that "Mercy
first and last shall brightest shine" (134).

Very much later in the poem, as divine grace succeeds in
restoring peace between the human pair on earth, Adam loses
all his anger (X.945) just as, in a sense, the Father has "lost"
His, and as Adam will see after the Flood that He forgets it
(XI.878). How complex a thing God's wrath is, and the whole

mystery of His ways to men, we are helped to sense more fully
at the end of Book X, when we hear Adam first reminding Eve
how God "both heard and judg'd/Without wrauth or reviling"
(1047–1048) and then, fifty lines further on, remembering
God's "look serene," in which "When angry most he seem'd and
most severe,/What else but favor, grace, and mercie shon?"
(1094–1096).

To introduce Adam to the divine mystery of wrath and
grace, and to draw him into the spiritual life of Christian heroism which the mystery offers, is the purpose of the revelation
given to him in vision and narrative. When he exclaims, "O
goodness infinite, goodness immense! . . . over wrauth grace
shall abound" (XII.469–478), he is coming to see and accept
what the narrator has foretold long before, at I.217–219; and in
his last speech (XII.553–573) he is entering upon a life characterized by that "better fortitude" (IX.31) which Milton had in
mind when he gave the narrator his lines about "Things unat-
tempted yet in Prose or Rhime" (I.13–16).[16]

Just before the prophetic visions begin, Michael says to
Adam,

> . . . *know I am sent*
> *To shew thee what shall come in future dayes*
> *To thee and to thy Ofspring; good with bad*
> *Expect to hear, supernal Grace contending*
> *With sinfulness of Men; thereby to learn*
> *True patience, and to temper joy with fear*
> *And pious sorrow, equally enur'd*
> *By moderation either state to beare,*
> *Prosperous or adverse: so shalt thou lead*
> *Safest thy life, and best prepar'd endure*
> *Thy mortal passage when it comes . . .*
> (XI.356–366)

This passage contains, one might say, the formula for the emotional quality of Adam's dramatic experience in the latter part

of the poem: "to temper joy with fear/And pious sorrow." In the end, all of these are present, complexly ordered in the emotions of Adam and Eve as they go into exile from the Paradise they have lost; by the time the poem reaches its conclusion, we have been brought to feel that all these diverse elements have to be accommodated in any conception of an adequate response to "the wrath of God." Adam and Eve do not lose the Garden until so much good that is unexpected and unmerited has been showered upon them that our ideas, and our consequent feelings, about wrath, death, and loss have all been — more than transposed; one might even say, transfigured.

Although the marvelous revelation comes very near to overwhelming Adam with joy, he does at last master the joy, as we have seen. The poem masters it too and, like Adam and Eve in the story, incorporates it with the primordial human pains of guilt and loss. To move the poem steadily toward that fusion is one of the chief esthetic functions of the last three dramatic speeches, that passage which gives us time to feel many tensions being brought into balance. The quieting movement attains its fruition with Eve's last words, which in reshaping yet once more the varied notes — "all . . . lost . . . favour . . . I unworthie . . . Promis'd . . . all restore" — complete the process of adjustment by which ecstatic joy becomes quiet, hopeful content not unmixed with pain. Her speech gives us the most complexly intimate glimpse the poem affords for any of its characters; obviously the epic cannot end there. So the narrator, a presence felt but lightly through most of Book XII, assumes a final brief prominence and gradually distances the characters, modulating from "our Mother *Eve*" to Adam to the Archangel, to the Cherubim "all in bright array," and the ordinary world's common laborer, on to the matchless close.

All the world loves it, though some have felt (as has been mentioned) that it does not really belong to Book XII, or follow dramatically from the joyous revelation. Surely that is a misunderstanding. It is imperative that the poem master the joy, because rebellion and crime, though forgiven, remain an indelible part of Adam's past and some of the consequences will continue to operate throughout all time; but also divine mercy, by encircling and permeating this human pain, has transformed it. Therefore all must be present in the end. So much of the power in the last four lines comes from what Milton does not there have to say, especially in "wandring" and "solitarie." The literal meanings give those words an obvious appropriateness. In more important ways, though, Adam and Eve are not "wandring," not "solitarie"; those other, nonexplicit, meanings, and our response to them, are what it has taken nearly all of Book XII, and in fact the whole poem, to develop. The two central characters are not themselves lost, although they have lost Paradise; and we may feel when we come to the poem's end that even the title itself is far richer in meaning than it seemed when we began. *Paradise Lost* narrates Milton's comforting vision of man's cosmic predicament. The complexity of tone at the end of it is the triumphant consummation of his epic intention to "assert Eternal Providence,/And justifie the ways of God to men" (I.25–26).

*An Essay for the Tercentenary
of 'Paradise Lost'*

I

Paradise Lost begins and ends with characters entering into exile: Satan and his followers expelled from Heaven, Adam and Eve exiled from Paradise. Coming full circle as it does, the poem recalls its beginning in its end, and the end may in addition remind us of the midpoint. For the conclusion of Book VI has also recalled the opening; the inset narrative ends by bringing us up to the situation as it was when the poem opened.

These facts are relevant to an idea I should like to discuss in this essay. Books XI and XII have often seemed unsatisfying because the prophetic visions and narratives — "an untransmuted lump of futurity," as C. S. Lewis called them[1] — have been felt to lack emotional power, and therefore to be imperfectly organic in the poem. Some attention to these sections over a number of years has left me persuaded that in fact they succeed much better than is commonly supposed. I should like to offer a hypothesis: when he made the change from a ten-book structure to the form of twelve books, Milton was trying (among other things) to make more obvious what he had all along intended us to understand as the poetic function of the revelation that Michael delivers to Adam.[2]

If Books XI and XII have more resonance than they have often been assumed to have, a natural place to look for links would be the midpoint of the poem. This means that when the poem had ten books, a reader of Book X might naturally find himself recalling details of Book V. Among various items of similarity and difference,[3] the most striking point of resemblance is obviously the fact that in both books an angel comes to visit Adam. Each of them comes by the gracious will of the Father, Raphael by narrating the past to give solemn warning in the midst of undisturbed joy, Michael by foretelling the future to diminish fear and pain with an intermixture of hope.[4]

But of course Raphael's narrative of the rebellion in Heaven, which does not begin even to get under way until the latter part of Book V, continues straight on into the next book and takes up the whole of it. Now the poem certainly reaches its midpoint with the end of the war in Heaven: 5,426 lines after the beginning (5,429 in 1674) in a total of 10,550 lines (10,565 in 1674). Even for the 1667 text Milton was thinking of the second structural half as opening with Book VII ("Half yet remaines unsung" — 21). Nevertheless, the effect is rather asymmetrical in a ten-book structure. When he rearranged the masses of his work into an order based on twelve structural units, he made the location of the exact center begin to function more poetically for our sense of the total architectonic harmony. I therefore suggest that one of his objects in changing to a twelve-book arrangement was to make even the mathematical dimensions of the poem reflect its explicit — and physical — division into two parts. By this simple strategy[5] he was able, without losing any of the resonances between Book V and the new Book XI,[6] to alert his readers that they should listen especially for resonances between the new Book XII and Book VI.

By separating the parts of Michael's revelation into two distinct books, Milton assists us to discriminate the appropriate links for the materials in each of the two modes of revelation. The visions, which constitute the first part of the revelation (XI.429–901), are linked chiefly with the early scenes in Hell — for the reason, it would appear, that antediluvian society was one hell of a world.[7] But Michael's narratives in Book XII are for the most part linked elsewhere. If, as we read them, we keep remembering that another angel was delivering another narrative in a book related by such precise mathematical proportion, we may find our way to correspondences important not only in the general outline but sometimes even in the detailed local texture.

Indeed, with the new lines he composed for the opening of Book XII (1–5) Milton gave us a clear signal to remember

Essay for the Tercentenary

the opening of Book VI (the references to a journey, and an angel). The Nimrod episode, being presented as the rise of tyranny on earth (32,39), may remind us of Satan's archetypal tyranny in Heaven;[8] and the subsequent philosophic interchange between Adam and Michael on rational liberty and right reason (63–101; cf. 29) recalls a variety of lines in Book VI, from the Father (41–42), from Abdiel (114–126, 172–188), and from Satan (164–170).

However, what we are chiefly meant to notice is the general *contrast* that Book XII makes with Book VI. Adam is behaving so differently from Satan, because the Father is handling Adam's rebellion so differently from the way He has treated Satan's. The first evidence that divine mercy is active within man appears when we see that Adam *can* respond differently from Satan. The process begins, of course, back in (new) Book X, with the restoration of harmony between Adam and Eve, and then their humble first gesture toward reunion with God. All this they can do because God has "remov'd/The stonie from thir hearts" (XI.3–4). When Michael reports the decree of expulsion from the Garden, Adam can say that "to his great bidding I submit" (XI.314) — an attitude radically different from Satan's self-assertive determination "never to submit or yield" (I.108). Throughout the visions of Book XI and the narratives of Book XII the operation of prevenient grace explains (theologically and psychologically) Adam's interested, receptive, grateful response to what Michael is revealing.

In Book XII, as Adam focuses attention chiefly on the idea of the Woman's Seed, he gradually learns that "hee, who comes thy Saviour" (393) is the same person that Raphael has already told him about, the Victor over Satan in the war in Heaven and the anointed Son of the Father. The fact that "son" is a key word throughout the Book (64, 80, 101, 145, 153, 155, 160, 161, 268, 327, 332, 357, 381, 388, 447, 448) helps to concentrate

73

attention on this character, and thereby to suggest that we remember how different the Son's role was in the earlier Book. We thus, along with Adam, learn to discriminate between the Son's two modes of victory. In Book VI He appeared in physical splendor and might (749–772); in Book XII, He is despised and rejected (404–419). Adam expects to hear about another physical combat and another physical victory over Satan (XII.384–385); he learns that, for the benefit of man, there is to be rather a *spiritual* victory over

> . . . *thy deaths wound:*
> *Which hee, who comes thy Saviour, shall recure,*
> *Not by destroying Satan, but his works*
> *In thee and in thy Seed: nor can this be,*
> *But by fulfilling that which thou didst want,*
> *Obedience to the Law of God, impos'd*
> *On penaltie of death, and suffering death,*
> *The penaltie to thy transgression due,*
> *And due to theirs which out of thine will grow:*
> *So onely can high Justice rest appaid.*
> (XII.392–401)[9]

Then the narrative leads on, through the crucifixion and resurrection and the subsequent gift of redemptive grace, to the idea of a spiritual warfare against evil that men who keep the faith (always few in number) will be enabled to prosecute — so different from the physical warfare between the angels in Book VI.[10]

But of course not all of the links for Book XII are with the war in Heaven of Book VI. A poem is an organism, so to speak, not just a set of abstract mathematical relations; once an item enters a poem, regardless of where it enters, it remains continuously present and operative. One striking illustration of the fact is a link between the end of Book V and Adam's last speech,

the great passage in which he responds to the revelation he has
received from Michael.

> *How soon hath thy prediction, Seer blest,*
> *Measur'd this transient World, the Race of time,*
> *Till time stand fixt: beyond is all abyss,*
> *Eternitie, whose end no eye can reach.*
> *Greatly instructed I shall hence depart,*
> *Greatly in peace of thought, and have my fill*
> *Of knowledge, what this Vessel can containe;*
> *Beyond which was my folly to aspire.*
> *Henceforth I learne, that to obey is best,*
> *And love with fear the onely God, to walk*
> *As in his presence, ever to observe*
> *His providence, and on him sole depend,*
> *Mercifull over all his works, with good*
> *Still overcoming evil, and by small*
> *Accomplishing great things, by things deemd weak*
> *Subverting worldly strong, and worldly wise*
> *By simply meek; that suffering for Truths sake*
> *Is fortitude to highest victorie,*
> *And to the faithful Death the Gate of Life;*
> *Taught this by his example whom I now*
> *Acknowledge my Redeemer ever blest.*
> (XII.553–573)

Hearing Adam speak these lines, we may feel that in a sense he
is choosing Abdiel's role for himself;[11] and in that item of poetic
structure Milton is retaining a link that perhaps would have
seemed more neatly, even mathematically, pleasing to readers
of his first edition. For the final episode of Book V is that in
which the faithful Abdiel indignantly rejects the invitation to
ally himself with Satan's rebellious forces. When Adam's last
speech came toward the close of (old) Book X, there was a
certain precise elegance to be enjoyed by remembering Abdiel's
scene at the very end of Book V. But in any event, whether

Adam's speech comes at the close of X or of XII, we can hardly miss the thematic import of the contrast within similarity if we compare the speech with the narrator's thrilling, muscular, but relatively simple rhythms in his praise for Abdiel's heroic stand:

> So spake the Seraph Abdiel *faithful found,*
> Among the faithless, faithful only hee;
> Among innumerable false, unmov'd,
> Unshak'n, unseduc'd, unterrifi'd
> His Loyaltie he kept, his Love, his Zeale;
> Nor number, nor example with him wrought
> To swerve from truth, or change his constant mind
> Though single. From amidst them forth he passd,
> Long way through hostile scorn, which he susteind
> Superior, nor of violence fear'd aught;
> And with retorted scorn his back he turn'd
> On those proud Towrs to swift destruction doom'd.
>   (V.896–907)

Set beside the splendid simplicity of this stirring passage, the inwardness and the complexity of tone in the subtle rhythms of Adam's speech bring home to us by contrast how great a distance the poem has traversed as it has narrated the story of Adam's loss.[12]

II

Abdiel's role, with which in effect Adam chooses to associate himself, is a specifically heroic mode of the spiritual life. We may also say, more generally, that this act of choice by Adam, toward which the poem as a whole has been moving, is the act by which he reenters spiritual life itself. Milton's structural revisions for the 1674 edition, by bringing out more sharply the relation between Book XII and Book VI, help us to perceive that as the essential character of Adam's experience.

The spirituality of his first state in the poem is that perfect integrity he originally enjoyed in which, as his supreme felicity, he was graced with unclouded friendship with God and in which, as the happy consequences of that, he was harmoniously related to his environment and also possessed within himself a wholeness characterized by harmony between the inward and the outward aspects of his own nature. The shape of Adam's overall experience can therefore be described as a movement from the felicitous harmony of this spiritual order, to the destruction of it, to his recovery of life in the inward man, a life made possible through the gift of spiritual regeneration. For Adam has to reenter spiritual life under the conditions of fallen humanity. The inward man, even when made alive again by regeneration, must now be separate from the outward; spirituality is no longer consonant with man's physical nature. By perceiving this development, we may also perceive the organically contrasting relation that Book XII has with other books besides the sixth, notably the fourth, from which we have received an unforgettable picture of Adam in his original integrity.[13]

In Milton's conception of Adam's story, and everybody else's, man can escape from disaster because rescue is offered to him. Adam enters the visions with a certain Pelagian tendency to self-dependence (XI.371–376); he learns that the rest he desires can be his only as a gift from God, but also that God is willing to give it. Adam's act of accepting the offer from God is what makes him the hero of the poem,[14] and it is profitable to consider several aspects of the heroic stature he achieves.

For one thing, when he explicitly accepts the Son as his Redeemer, he is believing before there is anybody else in the world except Eve to give him human companionship and support in the act of faith. It takes some bravery to be the first, especially in the total absence of human fellowship; and I think we may infer that in Milton's eyes Adam achieves heroic stature by being the first to make the leap into faith.

When he makes his choice of allegiance at the end, he is in effect entering upon a spiritual war, a peculiarly complex mode of conflict in which he both wins a victory over self and submits himself in humility to divine governance — or rather, he wins a victory over self by means of humble submission to God. Pride, the root cause of all sin, means that the creature is putting himself first — ethically, and in the long run, metaphysically. To acknowledge that one is not really first is not, perhaps, so very difficult simply as an intellectual act, even for fallen man; one might perceive the truth philosophically, and say it, yet still continue to live in pride. But effectively to accept the truth in practice means to take God as the guide of life, and that means to accept the divine initiative for all one's affairs. So much would be true for everyone simply by virtue of man's creaturehood, even if man had never sinned. Fallen man faces an additional complication. To admit that one needs help and to accept it — in the technical language of theology, to acknowledge one's need for *gratia sanans* — is perhaps the hardest thing of all for man fallen into pride, and even to do that much takes grace. Adam does all these things, difficult as they may be. He acknowledges his helplessness; he submits to the divine initiative; he accepts the Son as his Redeemer. By these several actions he accomplishes his renunciation of pride. He is the first of his race to do so, and apparently Milton wishes us to consider him a hero by virtue of his brave deed of self-mastery.

Adam nevertheless perceives that after sin has entered human experience, the true way of life is the way of endurance, of patience under affliction. To say that is to describe something of the poem's idea about the spiritual conflict that man is able to wage against evil — man endowed with grace, that is, for in this struggle man's action, necessarily subordinate, is always dependent on assistance from grace, and victory itself is always reserved to God. Sin being a foe so overwhelming, He is the only one who can defeat it; man's role must always be secondary, either doing or enduring, as God wills. Adam calls this way of life "suffering for Truths sake" and identifies it as "fortitude to highest victorie" (XII.569–570). Earlier, the narrator has called it "the better fortitude/Of Patience and Heroic Martyrdom" (IX.31–32).

Milton certainly is saying that the proper human role is the secondary one of response — to accept whatever situations the infinitely creative God presents (wonderfully surprising they are likely to prove), and to live within them in total dependence upon Him, including dependence upon His grace to deal with evil.[15] And Milton certainly is saying one thing more. From the evil that besets man there is only one possible route of escape. Only if God rescues him can he come out alive from the sundry and manifold dangers of the world; divine rescue is a categorical necessity, absolutely the condition of life for man. In the opinion of this poet, for a man to accept his true role of response, and to trust himself to the divine rescue, and to do all that from the posture of fallen humanity, is a heroic achievement. It takes grace, of course, as Milton always recognizes. But, if man accepts the proffered grace, the way is open for him to achieve a victory over self by humbly accepting whatever comes, doing whatever God guides him to do and suffering for Truth's sake if need be. In that way man may even have a share in the divine victory over evil.

The point of all this for literary criticism, for appreciation and judgment of the poem as a poem, is that Milton tries to help us *feel* this as the choice that Adam makes. We need not depend merely upon the words he explicitly uses. We really may sense the — strangely — heroic quality of his action, and we may even identify the source of the effect. In considerable measure it is that very strategy which has usually been judged so unsuccessful, Milton's literary style for the prophetic visions and narratives.

Most readers have felt that those sections, though containing some great moments, do not in general reach the heights to which the poem has accustomed us. In his *Preface to Paradise Lost,* C. S. Lewis even went so far as to say that "the actual writing in this passage is curiously bad" (p. 125), and Louis L. Martz has recently affirmed the same judgment about certain portions of Michael's narratives.[16] The passage seems to me to have, on the contrary, sustained power and beauty, and an organically poetic function which it succeeds very well in performing. To the adverse judgment one usually hears, the following comments may be offered in reply.

(1) Whatever measure of poetic excellence one credits in general to the long summary of Biblical history, as rhetoric it is superb — a terse, discriminating, economical condensation of huge masses of material.[17] Thematically, too, Milton remains in complete control throughout, the proof being that he consistently emphasizes what he wants to emphasize (as will be shown below).

(2) Some great moments certainly occur. Measured by the very highest artistic standards of even this poem, splendid passages of poetry keep turning up regularly, every one of them at a key point in the rhetorical and thematic structure (XI.749–762, 822–835; XII.307–314, 324–330, 368–371, 458–465, 537–551). A poet who can pull out the stops whenever he wants to has surely not lost control.

Furthermore, the succession of high points in Michael's narratives in Book XII makes up a sequence of climaxes whose function is to give with gradually increasing power a sense of how God will decisively intervene in human affairs to rescue man now that man cannot deliver himself. The climaxes move from the low-keyed passage about the arrival of Abraham's sons in their earthly Canaan (XII.260–269), through progressively more dazzling anticipations of the Redeemer (307–314, 368–371, 458–465), to the longest and most fervent of all (537–551), prophesying the Second Advent and the renewing of the whole creation. The effect of this sequence is to dramatize what was defined a moment ago as one of Milton's basic affirmations in *Paradise Lost.* Victory over evil is solely, and totally, God's; man is able, at most, to respond to a victory won for him by his Redeemer. The sequential ordering of these climactic passages, the skillfully paced *crescendo* in the poetic eloquence bestowed upon the materials — in a word, the specifically artistic design of Michael's narratives serves to body forth one of Milton's fundamental Christian insights.

(3) It is true that in the visions and prophetic narratives the language seems rather less impregnated with meaning than the usual character of Milton's diction has taught us to expect. Nevertheless, there are a number of detailed local resonances to be heard, especially in the visions, as has already been mentioned. In another way, too, we may usefully discriminate the visions from the narratives.

The visions are something apart, framed, as they should be. One senses a different quality in the verse, new here and unique in the poem (though it extends into Michael's narrative account of Nimrod, at the beginning of Book XII). It can be explained at least in part by the fact that material is being presented in rather shorter semantic units, with the consequence that in a sense we are being asked to receive more meaning than usual from each ten syllables.[18] There are many compound constructions (subjects, verbs, and objects); noticeable use is also made of inversions and elliptical constructions. By these varied means the visions communicate an impression of an exceptionally tough, vigorous mind that will make no concessions to us as listeners;

and, just as Adam himself is under great strain during the visions, probably we are meant to feel some corresponding sense
of strain as we try to grasp the large mass of varied detail being
offered so tersely.[19] In that respect this section of the poem succeeds in giving to us as readers an experience analogous to the
experience Adam is having as he watches the visions; and it
communicates to us with steadily increasing power, as the visions
communicate to Adam himself, the meaning of that death which
he is responsible for having introduced into the created world.

Beginning with the account of God's call to Abraham (XII.
105ff.), Michael's narratives return us to the ordinary manner
of the poem, except that now we feel an impoverishment in the
diction. At least three causes for this comparatively pale character
in the language may be identified. For one thing, Milton is
keeping the "inset" materials at a considerable distance. Adam's
dramatic experience is the action we remain close to; the prophecies to which he is listening are being kept at some remove from
us. And secondly, none of the human participants in the Biblical
story being prophetically narrated has been a character in the
action of *Paradise Lost*. Hence there can be no ties of sympathy,
no links to places or persons or events, though which the materials can be given depth and resonance by being related to our
memories of what has preceded in the poem. It would appear
that Milton nevertheless believes he can afford this sketchy,
allusive approach, and presumably because he knows he can
count on his readers' being familiar with the materials. They are
the traditions of the Christian readers for whom he is writing,
analogous to the materials of the roll-calls in earlier epics.

The most important contributing cause, however, is the
nature of the theme Milton has chosen to develop. What we experience poetically is exactly what Michael, before the visions
began, has told Adam he will hear about, "supernal Grace con-
tending/With sinfulness of Men" (XI.359–360). These are

brought into focus through the gradual revelation to Adam of the spiritual action by which the Son bruises Satan's head; and for these chief emphases it *is* possible, as has been shown, to provide an enriching structure of links with earlier sections of the poem. Milton is bringing all the narrative materials together by means of these unifying threads in order to give us an image of that spiritual mode of life toward which Adam's experience in the revelation is moving him and which at the end he solemnly accepts as his own.

It is a fearfully difficult theme to manage poetically. It does not readily accommodate itself to the image-making faculty because in the spiritual conflict between human sin and divine grace, human action must be subordinate and the divine action cannot be directly visible. By definition, therefore, this poet can have no images for the supreme role (except in such portions of the narrative as deal with the Incarnate Son). And yet for Milton the "spiritual" is supremely real, exciting, and alive, incomparably the most valuable dimension available to human experience. Therefore he wishes, being a poet, to communicate his feeling for its vitality — even though for many years the inaccessibility of the spiritual to the senses has been one of his cardinal principles. Here, in fact, he is trying to make poetry out of that same conception of "spiritual" which twenty-five years earlier he had begun to expound rhetorically in the antiepiscopal tracts; and it springs from the same impulse in the interpretation of Biblical religion, an impulse to repudiate all liturgical vesture and all overt formalism because such things are believed to profane and falsify the invisible, inward purity of spiritual reality.[20]

The ultimate reason for such a belief, apparently, is a belief that the fall weakened human sense calamitously. It had not always been so weak. In the original state of integrity Adam's physical nature and his material environment could each have its share in that single unified reality which could be called quite literally "spiritual." [21] Hence the physical richness in such passages as the descriptions of the Garden and of man's life within it (IV.132–165, 205–355, 610–775; V.266–349), and the canticle of praise in Book V (153–208). True, Adam even in his innocence could not physically sustain the presence of God for very long (VIII.452–459). But he could sustain it on occasion (cf.XI.315–327), and the whole of his nature could share in the experience. Now that the original harmony has been destroyed and man's outward physical nature consequently weakened, "objects divine/Must needs impaire and wearie human sense" (XII.9–10).[22] Milton believes that under grace in the present dispensation man is being renewed, but only in the inward part; the restoration of total integrity will come later.[23] Nevertheless, his lively sense of what inward spirituality means is what he is chiefly trying to communicate through his poetic manner in the prophetic narratives.

At this late moment in his poem, then, Milton is making his climactic gesture, the poetic act for which everything before has been preparation. For it he wants a style that will distinguish itself by virtue of the contrast it makes with the dominant style of what has preceded. Far from being the consequence of haste, or fatigue, or flagging interest, or old age, or weakened sensibility, or lack of helpful criticism, or whatever other deficiency one may name, the poetic manner of Michael's narratives results from a very deliberate choice. The artistic success of this manner — if we decide it is success — derives chiefly from the sound; and indeed Michael's narratives, through the sustained power of their rhythm and cadence, are unfailingly melodious. I should not wish to be without a single line of them, if for no other reason than that they enlarge our store of the ravishing Miltonic sound. This poet's mature verse possesses everywhere, in cadence and rhythm together, a Mozartean sweetness, opulence, and energy that make it, to my ear, the most beautiful music in English.

Dispensing in the main with his usual richness of detailed contextual resonances, Milton sets out to make even the impoverished diction of Michael's narratives work for him poetically. He builds partly upon the plain literal sense of what is said, partly — and very largely — upon the sound-structure of his verse. The result is an effect of remarkable complexity, involving at least three clearly distinguishable components. To begin with, the verse is reflecting what Adam's world has come to; Michael's narratives are poetry about a fallen world. If we feel that in some ways they are rather thin stuff poetically, we are responding just the way Milton wants; the narratives are saying that Adam's world now, the fallen world we all know, looks like this.[24] But also, statements about the persistent intervention of supernal grace are continually turning up, repeatedly intermixing their own reflections of its light and life with the outward dullness of passages about the merely human scene (111–113, 120–126, 147–148, 170–171, 200–205, 208–210, 227–230, 245–248, 307–314, 324–330, 345–347, 358–371, 419–435, 450, 458–465, 485–502, 539–551). For this poetry about a fallen world is poetry about a world that God is redeeming, and first of all with renewed life for the inward man. So, thirdly and chiefly, Milton is trying also to show us what the "spiritual" is like. To that end his means are chiefly aural and kinesthetic.[25] I should argue that the prophetic narratives do succeed in giving us an image of the spiritual life to which God is recalling Adam: a sense of its inward nature by the relatively pale character of the diction, and simultaneously a sense of its vitality and ever-renewed freshness by the marvelous variety and power in the rhythm.[26]

The whole of this effect was intended and in all essentials was achieved from the first, in the ten-book version of 1667. The latter portion of its final book contained all the components of the effect; and Michael's prophetic narratives possessed then, just as they possess now, that organic relation with Raphael's earlier narrative of the war in Heaven by which the poetic significance of the prophetic narratives is so much clarified. Only, the relation itself was not so effectively signalled as it might have been. The second edition of 1674 both is and is not the same poem. There is an almost identical text, with almost the same number of lines; and most of the chief structural units have been left intact. For two of the original blocks, however, Milton has effected a reshaping, designed, in part, to enhance the artistic impact of what had been an organizing theme from the first. The nature of that spiritual life to which God restores Adam, and its character in the heroic mode of it that Adam chooses for himself, are illuminated for our imagination as we think about the special relation between Books VI and XII; and what now may stimulate us to perceive the relation very clearly is the structure as Milton finally determined it for the revised edition of his poem. By such means, it would appear, he was trying to make *Paradise Lost* more accessible for readers as a poem doctrinal and exemplary to a nation.

The Rhythm of 'Paradise Lost,'
Books XI and XII

The Conflict of Paradise Lost

Books XI & XII

I

Something quite wonderful emerges when the first 125 lines of *Paradise Lost* XI are read aloud. The narrator begins *allegretto* and *piano* with twenty-one lines that prolong the quietness from Book X just concluded. Next the Son offers to the Father the prayers of Adam and Eve, in a speech also quiet, urgent yet firmly confident, a speech that kinesthetically suggests upward movement of eyes and arms, the very shape of priestly intercession.

The great surprise comes in the Father's two speeches. There is no bluster at all. The verse guides one to reduce greatly both tempo and volume and then to sustain the levels established, with scarcely the slightest variation. The first speech (46–71), delivered privately to the Son, is almost whispered, a subdued *legato* of most delicate nuance — tender, wistful, regretful, even pained. "I at first with two fair gifts/Created him endowd" (57–58): the Father sounds like a venerable and benevolent human trying to understand how gifts bestowed in pure love could have been so despised. The same note pervades His second, public, speech (84–125), right to the end:

> *Least Paradise a receptable prove*
> *To Spirits foule, and all my Trees thir prey,*
> *With whose stol'n Fruit Man once more to delude.*
> (XI.123–125)

The first two of these lines suggest the feeling of a person who has made something infinitely beautiful for another's joy, only to see it trampled and profaned in sheer malice; the last is like a father working to shield his disappointing child from a really vicious danger. This whole complex feeling is present at the most official moments of the speech:

> *. . . to remove him I decree,*
> *And send him from the Garden forth to Till*

The Ground whence he was taken, fitter soile.

. . . .

Hast thee, and from the Paradise of God
Without remorse drive out the sinful Pair,
From hallowd ground th' unholie, and denounce
To them and to thir Progenie from thence
Perpetual banishment . . .

(XI.96–108)

The skillful way the lines have been shaped points up the grave solemnity of what is being done, but they are not spoken emphatically. They are neither loud, nor biting, nor stentorian; muted, rather, and regretful, though firm.

The suppressed quality of the sound in the opening runs into the contrast of Adam's sprightlier rhythms (141–161) at the beginning of the next scene. Only for a moment, though; Eve's practical soul, burdened with shame and humiliation, is already feeling weighted down by the work to be done before she and Adam return to dust. Her speech (163–180), slower and more quiet, brings back with a difference something of the quietness and the pain we have been hearing. Milton is working toward the much louder volume with which the book will close; he therefore begins from the opposite end of the scale. He is also working toward the quiet, subdued complexities with which the whole poem will end, thereby to produce a balance of likenesses that are yet unlike — a structural pattern that was probably more obvious when XI and XII made one single book.

These remarks may suggest something of the way Milton senses the values of his theme and story. Sound, more for this poet than for most, constitutes the fundamental, essential medium for poetic exploration and perception. Rhythm is a most important key to *Paradise Lost*; tempo and volume are the chief instruments for controlling an extraordinary range of rhythmic effects. Milton *hears* his values, in the double sense that hearing is centrally important in itself, and also that it is commonly a means through which he achieves other imaginative sensations.[1] And no reader need fear difficulty in trying to perceive the rhythmic effects; the cues are all built in.

II

After Michael has completed the preliminaries of his mission (XI.238–376), he ascends with Adam "In the Visions of God" (377). From that point on to the end of Book XI, we hear three voices. The visions themselves are presented by the relatively impersonal narrator, whose *allegro* pace, not very loud usually, is the rhythmic norm of the whole poem. The characters' speeches, here as elsewhere, tend to be somewhat slower than the narrator's parts. Adam carries the emotional response to the visions, deeply felt, vigorously expressed, and, speaking generally, scaled in a pattern of gradually rising intensity. Michael's speech is *allegretto,* not so loud as Adam's but louder than the narrator's, syntactically and emotionally generalized, a suitably detached mode for instructing Adam in the religious meanings of the revelation. For revelation, in the technical sense of that word, is what Michael is delivering to Adam: not just a certain group of events, but also the divine purpose and meaning in the events.

So we have this pattern: first the narrator's rapid sketch, followed by Adam's slower response, increasingly passionate as the experience deepens, and last Michael's pedagogic firmness and efficiency.[2] Then the verse bounds ahead once more as the narrator offers another pictorial narrative, and the sequence is under way again.

That is a fair sketch of the normative rhythmic pattern that establishes itself, though with innumerable subtle variations, from line 429, where the first vision begins, through about line 682, the end of Adam's response to the (fourth) vision of war and the rescue of Enoch. Thereafter, as both angel and man are more and more caught up in the visions of God, the tonal pattern develops greater complexities. Michael seems to become, one would not quite say more interested, but more involved. The jaw-breaking first sentence of his speech at 683, jammed with plosives and labials, realizes his sense of the frustration inevitable for those who choose to violate the moral constitution of reality, and also a sense of disgust with them. The next dozen lines, about false heroism, he delivers with some heat; then, gradually slowing the pace and raising the volume from 700 to 710, he realizes a sense of wonder as he contemplates the surprising, the amazing redemptive action of God:

> But hee the seventh from thee, whom thou beheldst
> The onely righteous in a World perverse,
> And therefore hated, therefore so beset
> With Foes for daring single to be just,
> And utter odious Truth, that God would come
> To judge them with his Saints: Him the most High
> Rapt in a balmie Cloud with winged Steeds
> Did, as thou sawst, receave, to walk with God
> High in Salvation and the Climes of bliss,
> Exempt from Death; to shew thee what reward
> Awaits the good, the rest what punishment . . .
> (XI.700–710)

The first 5.6 lines develop the ostensible grammatical subject; then the sentence moves off again to a new start, with a grammatical inversion ("Him the most High"), followed by a modifying line. Now comes the verb, its two words separated by the short clause that operates to engage Adam personally, with the consequence that "receave," the key word toward which the whole sentence has been working, sounds at the precise center of its line, its prominence emphasized syntactically, dramatically, and rhythmically. A great rise in pitch, signifying Michael's strong excitement and emphasized by the initial trochee ("High in"), follows in the next line, after which the doctrinal inference ("to shew thee," etc.) gracefully relaxes some of the tension.[3] Michael knows God, what He can do, what He is going to do; and yet when it is done, it never ceases to be marvelous in his eyes. Milton, one is tempted to believe, is remembering that the gospel is something "the angels desire to look into" (1 Pet. i.12), and perhaps it was in that text that he found a hint for the gradual rise in ardent joy and wonder which is the course along which Michael's experience develops from here to the end of the poem.

Before the story of redemption can begin, however, Michael has to exhibit the punishment of the antediluvian wicked. The progressive vision of death that unifies the first five visions now approaches its climax. The narrator's voice begins in the usual way (712), then at 733 ("when loe a wonder strange!") starts introducing his own tonal variation: his sense of marvel, hence his dramatic involvement. This small — and, in a way, antici-patory — action quickly comes to its climax at 737 —

> . . . *and God made fast the dore*

— the tempo somewhat retarded within a sharply *staccatto* enunciation. With the next line the *allegro* norm resumes but gradually reduces itself as the volume rises straight toward the rather slow, and very loud, passage:

> . . . *Sea cover'd Sea,*
> *Sea without shoar; and in thir Palaces*
> *Where luxurie late reign'd, Sea-monsters whelp'd*
> *And stabl'd; of Mankind, so numerous late,*
> *All left, in one small bottom swum imbark't.*
> (XI.749–753)

Precisely now, and for the first time in these visions, the narrator permits himself a gesture of close emotional community with Adam as he addresses him directly:

93

> *How didst thou grieve then,* Adam, *to behold*
> *The end of all thy Ofspring, end so sad,*
> *Depopulation . . .*
>   (XI.754–756)

"Depopulation" — Latinate, polysyllabic, emphatically placed in
the midst of all those simpler words: it carries a sense of the
relentless sweeping away of everything.

Adam's complete hopelessness, his crushed sense of mankind's final and total annihilation, makes itself heard in the
slow, listless monotones of his next speech (763–786). The
flood does, so to speak, bring about the dissolution of mankind;
in Adam's eyes it consummates the sentence he has heard God
pass upon himself. It must be brought home to him with unforgettable force, so Michael narratively delivers a second, powerful, account of it, emphasizing in his usual way the moral and
religious content of the revelation. Like the narrator's before
it, this version gradually becomes slower and louder. In that
manner we hear the powerfully evocative, much-admired lines
829–835 (ending with "an Iland salt and bare,/The haunt of
Seales and Orcs, and Sea-mews clang"); but they are not the
climax. That comes last with the religious point, abstractly
worded, fairly slow, firm and moderately loud, extremely austere
and demanding:

> *To teach thee that God attributes to place*
> *No sanctitie, if none be thither brought*
> *By Men who there frequent, or therein dwell.*
>   (XI.836–838)

After the rainbow and Adam's joy, we *hear* Michael smile
("Dextrously thou aim'st — 884). He draws the last speech
more and more into predominantly iambic cadences, the great
C Major of the poem, and thus leads the book to its conclusion
in a firm and stately tempo that rounds out the visions with a
glowing sense of finality:

Such grace shall one just Man find in his sight,
That he relents, not to blot out mankind,
And makes a Covenant never to destroy
The Earth again by flood, nor let the Sea
Surpass his bounds, nor Rain to drown the World
With Man therein or Beast; but when he brings
Over the Earth a Cloud, will therein set
His triple-colour'd Bow, whereon to look
And call to mind his Cov'nant: Day and Night,
Seed time and Harvest, Heat and hoary Frost
Shall hold thir course, till fire purge all things new,
Both Heav'n and Earth, wherein the just shall dwell.
(XI.890–901)[4]

III

During the prophetic narratives of Book XII the narrator's voice drops away almost completely. Adam continues to exhibit strong emotional responses that steadily rise in fervent excitement up through the speech at 469ff. ("O goodness infinite . . . full of doubt I stand"). In the great retardation there we can sense the questing, probing activity of his mind, grateful and overwhelmed, as he labors to comprehend the marvels he has been hearing about. Then at 479 the slow pace of musing suddenly gives way (as before at 384–385) to the brisk tempo of his eager questions.

Michael's second narrative is much the longest of his five, 165 lines even if we count only from line 105; actually the speech as a whole contains 191 lines (79–269). One feels it must strain any artist to keep up the impression of life in a single voice going on for so long. A wonderfully alert sense for variations in tempo is what Milton chiefly depends on for his success here.

The disheartening story of Nimrod, with its aftermath for human life generally, leads Michael to his disgusted, perhaps even bored, summary rhythms of 105–106:

> *Thus will this latter, as the former World,*
> *Still tend from bad to worse . . .*

Then his interest and his zest spring up afresh with the story of God's redemptive acts. At 111 and 113, tempo retards, enunciation becomes sharp and emphatic, as Michael's mind begins to grow fascinated in wonder at what God can do:

> *And one peculiar Nation to select*
> *From all the rest, of whom to be invok'd,*
> *A Nation from one faithful man to spring . . .*

There is a passionate outburst, *allegro*, from 115 to 120, intimately addressed to Adam personally:

> *. . . O that men*
> *(Canst thou believe?) should be so stupid grown,*
> *While yet the Patriark liv'd, who scap'd the Flood,*
> *As to forsake the living God, and fall*
> *To worship thir own work in Wood and Stone*
> *For Gods! . . .*

then the story resumes and almost at once comes to a fine climax, spoken with some grandeur:

> *. . . and upon him showre*
> *His benediction so, that in his Seed*
> *All Nations shall be blest . . .*
> (XII.124–126)

Fast tempo returns with the very energetic "he straight obeys" (126), after which we have about twenty lines of geography, done with very pleasing dramatic vivaciousness. All along through these lines we are hearing Michael's (and Milton's) sense of wonder, which comes to its next local climax at 147–148, very grand and solemn:

> *This pon der, that all Na tions of the Earth*
> *Shall in his Seed be bless ed . . .*

Faster, narrative tempos come back at 151 ("This Patriarch blest,/Whom *faithful Abraham* due time shall call") and lead on to the superb *bravura* passage 173–190, all ten plagues of Egypt in one single overwhelming sentence. These lines steadily pick up speed and volume through 188; then comes a sharp, sudden reduction of pace, the volume rising:

> *Last with one midnight stroke all the first-born*
> *Of Egypt must lie dead* . . .
> (XII.189–190)

The speech runs on for eighty lines more, continually adjusting tempo and volume in this now familiar way, and reaching several local climaxes. Then a curious thing happens. Here is how the very long speech ends:

> . . . *the rest*
> *Were long to tell, how many Battels fought,*
> *How many Kings destroyd, and Kingdoms won,*
> *Or how the Sun shall in mid Heav'n stand still*
> *A day entire, and Nights due course adjourne,*
> *Mans voice commanding, Sun in Gibeon stand,*
> *And thou Moon in the vale of* Aialon,
> *Till* Israel *overcome; so call the third*
> *From* Abraham, *Son of* Isaac, *and from him*
> *His whole descent, who thus shall* Canaan *win.*
> (XII.260–269)

Both syntax and sound are important here. ". . . the rest/Were long to tell" suggests that there are huge masses of material which Michael simply does not want to bother with. The next clauses, though regular iambs, perhaps may impel one to rush through dactylically: "hów mănў Battels fought,/ Hów mănў Kings destroyd." Then comes the great miracle, very much played down: grammatically paired ("Or how") with the hurried summary just preceding, a human creature's amazing act minimized into an absolute phrase ("Mans voice commanding"), a supremely important name tacked on at the end in a short adverbial clause ("Till *Israel* overcome"), the last triumphant word ("win") placed in another modifying clause, the whole spoken in a rather nondescript, unimpressive tone of voice. No other speech in the poem ends that way.

There is a good reason for this; a minimum of emphasis is what Milton wants just at this point. Not very loud, not very emphatic, the passage yet has the note of a victory given by God. Adam is unaware, but Milton is counting on his audience to remember, that the man who gives orders to the sun is *"Joshua* whom the Gentiles *Jesus* call" (310), Joshua a type of Jesus. Adam does not yet know who the Woman's Seed is, nor does he know that the man Jesus will also be God. He does not know, either, that the miracle he is hearing about is really a divine act of rescue: "And there was no day like that before it or after it, that the Lord hearkened unto the voice of a man: for the Lord fought for Israel" (Joshua x.14). Milton has chosen the incident, and presented it, with the greatest possible care. For it is essential to, very precisely, the *poetic* effect of the whole that exactly at this point Adam should understand but dimly while we perceive everything. What he hears about is some wonderful event, "Mans voice commanding." He does not know, but Milton expects us to know, that this is one man, a type of Man, participating in a divine act of rescue, a redemption which is the divine answer to man's continuous and apparently hopeless degeneration.

For some time now Adam has been hearing about the surprising ways of God, who rescues Abraham from idolatry and Israel from slavery in Egypt, who sends fearful plagues to Pharaoh and gives miraculous powers to Moses at the Red Sea, who comes Himself to Sinai to "Ordaine them Lawes" (230), who even

The Rhythm of 'Paradise Lost'

. . . voutsafes
Among them to set up his Tabernacle,
The holy One with mortal Men to dwell . . .
                    (XII.246–248)[5]

Also, however, Adam has been hearing about heroic men: one faithful man from whom will rise "A mightie Nation" (124), two brothers "sent from God to claime/His people from enthralment" (170–171), the "potent Rod" of Moses (211), "Mans voice commanding" (265), Abraham's "whole descent, who thus shall *Canaan* win" (269). God rescues, consequently Man triumphs. This cannot be very clear to Adam; it is intended not to be, until the narrative of the Incarnation makes it possible to fuse the two themes. When he learns about that, Adam will truly begin to understand: "So God with man unites" (382).[6] For the present, though, he cannot see what it all means exactly, and that is what Milton is causing the verse to enact. The nondescript, unemphatic conclusion is obviously temporary; almost of itself the sound alone would compel Adam to listen for something more. It thus helps to keep him from thinking of the land of Canaan as the final goal. Canaan is no more than a promised land on earth, the dim foreshadowing of a greater glory soon to be revealed; so Michael will not encourage Adam to pause over it for very long. The conclusion works its effect upon us too. Michael sounds very perfunctory indeed; even if we had never heard of the Old Testament, we should know from the sound that his story is not yet finished.

His next speech, roughly half as long as the preceding, has two high points. The opening discourse on law moves at a steadily brisk pace to line 306, when the tempo slows for the extraordinary imaginative expansion at 307–314, where both abstract doctrine and the narrative point we have reached in the story are caught up for one splendid moment in a total cosmic vision ("and bring back/Through the worlds wilderness long wanderd man/Safe to eternal Paradise of Rest"). Immediately thereafter Michael resumes the fast narrative norm and moves through a deft summary of Old Testament history (quite as efficient in its way as the discourse on law just before) to the short climax at the end: a retard at 368–369, as Michael tries to realize the mystery of the Incarnation, and then a slightly quicker pace as he presents a brief glimpse of Christ the King:

> *A Virgin is his Mother, but his Sire*
> *The Power of the most High; he shall ascend*
> *The Throne hereditarie, and bound his Reign*
> *With earths wide bounds, his glory with the Heav'ns.*
> (XII.368–371)

The fourth narrative begins to come into rhythmic focus right at its center:

> *. . . so he dies,*   419
> *But soon revives, Death over him no power*   420
> *Shall long usurp; ere the third dawning light*   421
> *Returne, the Starres of Morn shall see him rise*   422
> *Out of his grave, fresh as the dawning light,*   423
> *Thy ransom paid, which Man from death redeems,*   424
> *His death for Man . . .*   425

— first the short summary clauses in 419–421; then the surging, soaring energies of 421–423; into slower, louder rhythms for the doctrine of 424–425. The verse moves on to the slow, loud, emphatic, and triumphant revelation of 427–429,

> *. . . this God-like act*
> *Annuls thy doom, the death thou shouldst have dy'd,*
> *In sin for ever lost from life . . .*

through a series of lines enunciated with a strong sense of very strenuous, even fierce, muscularity,

The Rhythm of 'Paradise Lost'

>   . . . this act
> Shall bruise the head of Satan, crush his strength
> Defeating Sin and Death, his two maine armes,
> And fix farr deeper in his head thir stings
> Then temporal death shall bruise the Victors heel . . .
>   (XII.429–433)

and then modulates into the serene *allegretto* cadences of 434–435:

> Or theirs whom he redeems, a death like sleep,
> A gentle wafting to immortal Life.

A brief historical and doctrinal summary (436–449), generally in the *allegro* norm, ends in the suddenly slow and majestic

> So in his seed all Na tions shall be blest.
>   (450)

The heroic triumph over Satan (451–455) is told in fast and powerful tempos, and these are followed by a gradual retard (with no diminution of volume) for the elaborate vision of judgment and a redeemed creation:

>   . . . and thence shall come,
> When this worlds disolution shall be ripe,
> With glory and power to judge both quick and dead,
> To judge th' unfaithful dead, but to reward
> His faithful, and receave them into bliss,
> Whether in Heav'n or Earth, for then the Earth
> Shall all be Paradise, far happier place
> Then this of Eden, and far happier daies.
>   (XII.458–465)

Before the visions started, Michael told Adam,

>   . . . good with bad
> Expect to hear, supernal Grace contending
> With sinfulness of Men . . .
>   (XI.358–360)

The underlying pessimism of the last books, forecast here and often commented on by interpreters, can be felt most acutely in the very different final narrative, that extremely Puritan version of church history. A tremendous energy of vehement indignation against the "grievous Wolves" (508) achieves its most intense, emphatic concentration in this *stretta* passage, laced with fricatives and labials and, especially, aspirates:

> . . . *What will they then*
> *But force the Spirit of Grace it self, and binde*
> *His consort Libertie; what, but unbuild*
> *His living Temples, built by Faith to stand,*
> *Thir own Faith not anothers: for on Earth*
> *Who against Faith and Conscience can be heard*
> *Infallible? yet many will presume:*
> *Whence heavie persecution shall arise*
> *On all who in the worship persevere*
> *Of Spirit and Truth; the rest, farr greater part,*
> *Will deem in outward Rites and specious formes*
> *Religion satisf'd; Truth shall retire*
> *Bestuck with slandrous darts, and works of Faith*
> *Rarely be found . . .*
> (XII.524–537)

One arrives at this point breathless and exhausted, so that Michael's weary cadences in the next few lines seem exactly right:

> . . . *so shall the World goe on,*
> *To good malignant, to bad men benigne,*
> *Under her own waight groaning . . .*
> (XII.537–539)

They correspond to his rhythms earlier, at 105–106; and once again the listless monotony of sound and cadence gives way to a rebirth of energy as the thought moves from man's helplessness to the divine act of rescue. As Michael ends his last, most ecstatic treatment of the consummation of all things, he stretches out grammar and meaning and sound to suggest an eternity of joy:

> *New Heav'ns, new Earth, Ages of endless date*
> *Founded in righteousness and peace and love*
> *To bring forth fruits Joy and eternal Bliss.*
> (XII.549–551)

Three beautiful arias conduct the scene to its perfect close, each one individual and unique, most sensitively defined in cadence and tempo, volume, pitch, and syntax. Adam starts very slow, a mind trying to master enormous waves of joy and wonder; and as his emotions begin to come under control (about 560–561), he advances the tempo just slightly, though his speech remains throughout the slowest of the three. There is a striking predominance everywhere of light front vowels;[7] the gravity comes from the sure, stately poise toward which he is moving, which he achieves in the third, last, very long sentence (561–573). Michael answers to that poise in the firm, sustained movement of his one long sentence (575–587), keyed to a deeper voice than Adam's[8] and paced slightly faster. It carries the sense that in the revelation, totally bestowed and totally received, every conceivable obstacle has been surmounted; and though still elaborately formal, it perfectly counterbalances with the ardent glow of its music and idea all of Michael's earlier sharpness. "Let us descend now therefore," he goes on (588), and the diminishing intensities of sound begin to perform a descent.

Eve's personal, domestic, intimate speech, shortest of the three, is ordered into two sentences:

> *Whence thou returnst, and whither wentst, I know;* 610
> *For God is also in sleep, and Dreams advise,*
> *Which he hath sent propitious, some great good* 612
> *Presaging, since with sorrow and hearts distress*
> *Wearied I fell asleep: but now lead on;* 614

In mee is no delay; with thee to goe,
Is to stay here; without thee here to stay,   616
Is to go hence unwilling; thou to mee
Art all things under Heav'n, all places thou,   618
Who for my wilful crime art banisht hence.
This further consolation yet secure   620
I carry hence; though all by mee is lost,
Such favour I unworthie am voutsaft,   622
By mee the Promis'd Seed shall all restore.

The verbal simplicity of the middle part (614–619), in tension with the delicate complexities of the cadence, is sheltered between two sets of lines (610–614, 620–623) rather more exalted in diction; throughout the speech, high front vowel sounds interlace with sonorous ones.[9]

The section as a whole, three speeches and the narrative connections, takes up seventy-two lines, time enough for each character to articulate in leisured amplitude the ultimate emotions of his own experience, time enough too for us the audience to feel many poetic tensions being brought into dynamic balance. After a continuously varied agitation of sound for over five hundred lines, the control sustained through the entire length of this final part suggests the undecorated recapitulation of a theme after a strenuous cadenza. By the subtle elaboration of its design Milton achieves a sense of order restored, in the soul, in the family, and in the race.

Miltonic Sensibility in 'Paradise Lost'

I

One good way of getting to appreciate any work of art in its unique particularity is to define the sensibility that in it is responding to the materials being presented. In this essay I shall try to identify the action of Milton's sensibility in *Paradise Lost,* a wonderfully alert and supple responsiveness which, in holding together all the varied materials of the poem, contributes importantly to the achievement of the distinctive quality we all feel.[1] The subject may be approached by way of a glance at the narrator and the Father, two characters who have occasioned much difficulty for interpretation.

The narrator's is the first voice we hear in the poem, and the last. He is a persona, not Milton. He is a character — not in the story, of course, like Adam and Eve and the rest — but in the poem: an imagined character, the narrator, a blind poet fallen on evil days, religiously assisting now at the narration of this epic action.[2] He speaks a little more than a third of the poem (34.95+ per cent of the 10,565 lines).[3] He is thus a part of the poem's total economy, one among many means for so distributing the energies of response that the mind of Milton the poet, and of us who follow him, may achieve an order of a very definite and distinctive quality.

One consequence follows, of the greatest importance. Nothing at all is proved (about Milton's alleged indifference, insensitivity, emotional incoherence, fatigue) when we hear some unemphatic verses from the narrator after a passionate, vividly realized speech by one of the characters in the story.

> *So spake th' Apostate Angel, though in pain,*
> *Vaunting aloud, but rackt with deep despare . . .*
> (I.125–126)

thus the narrator after Satan's first speech (I.84–124); or again, after his speech at IV.358–392:

> So spake the Fiend, and with necessitie,
> The Tyrants plea, excus'd his devilish deeds.
> (IV.393–394)

The narrator is in the poem, not the story, and his voice comes to us from an angle different from that of the story's characters. His norm is fast and not very loud; the characters tend to speak more slowly, and often considerably louder. So when on some occasions (not all) we hear the narrator's rather neutral tone and his brisk but unexcited pace commenting morally or theologically, we should understand simply that this is a part of the total proportioning Milton is working out in order to make a poem. The moral and theological comments are often pale because he intends them to be so; only by being unemphatic can they perform their proper action in the total structure of energy that is the poem.

Not that the narrator is unmoved, even in such moments. Take a somewhat longer passage:

> So stretcht out huge in length the Arch-fiend lay
> Chain'd on the burning Lake, nor ever thence
> Had ris'n or heav'd his head, but that the will
> And high permission of all-ruling Heaven
> Left him at large to his own dark designs,
> That with reiterated crimes he might
> Heap on himself damnation, while he sought
> Evil to others, and enrag'd might see
> How all his malice serv'd but to bring forth
> Infinite goodness, grace and mercy shewn
> On Man by him seduc't, but on himself
> Treble confusion, wrath and vengeance pour'd.
> (I.209–220)

In these deliberately unemphatic lines we can hear a powerful response. By means of the narrator, talking this way, at this moment of the whole, Milton is articulating an attitude of wonder, of marvel even, at two things: the malice of Satan,

which never ceases to amaze him, and the awesome mystery he
perceives in the will of God, which so strangely allows this freedom to Satan, and this blessing to man.[4] All this Milton *hears,*
and so we hear it, through the rhythms and meanings of the
narrator's lines.

Amazement at the malice of all the devils, and more particularly at their blasphemous daring, works itself out on a very
large scale in Book I, beginning in the lines just before the
roll-call:

> *Nor had they yet among the Sons of Eve*
> *Got them new Names, till wandring ore the Earth,*
> *Through Gods high sufferance for the tryal of man,*
> *By falsities and lyes the greatest part*
> *Of Mankind they corrupted to forsake*
> *God thir Creator, and th' invisible*   369
> *Glory of him that made them, to transform*
> *Oft to the Image of a Brute, adorn'd*   371
> *With gay Religions full of Pomp and Gold,*
> *And Devils to adore for Deities . . .*
>   (I.364–373)

In 369–370 there are astonishment and incredulity, which move
into the disgust of 371, and end with the shudder in 373. This,
the organizing attitude of the entire roll-call, may be illustrated
by a single long sentence:

> *The chief were those who from the Pit of Hell*
> *Roaming to seek thir prey on earth, durst fix*
> *Thir Seats long after next the Seat of God,*
> *Thir Altars by his Altar, Gods ador'd*
> *Among the Nations round, and durst abide*
> *Jehovah thundring out of Sion, thron'd*
> *Between the Cherubim; yea, often plac'd*
> *Within his Sanctuary it self thir Shrines,*
> *Abominations; and with cursed things*
> *His holy Rites, and solemn Feasts profan'd,*
> *And with thir darkness durst affront his light.*
>   (I.381–391)

Physical recoil from deadly menace is enacted with the words "Pit," "Roaming," and "prey." The devils' hard brazenness literally makes itself heard in "durst . . . durst . . . durst" (echoed again in "cursed"). The entire sentence of eleven lines is one long stretch of emotion, carefully, characteristically, elaborated and intensified to reach its highest pitch, in sound as well as feeling, with the word *"self,"* a little more than two-thirds of the way through.

The narrator's speech typically moves from a fast, quiet beginning, fairly high in pitch, through a very gradual (sometimes only slight) retard, to a substantially lower pitch, at the end of a long sentence, or passage of several sentences. Occasionally the volume may rise during this process, more often not.[5] This speaker also moves easily through a considerable range of variation within certain fundamental attitudes.

> . . . *Thou from the first*
> *Wast present, and with mighty wings outspread*
> *Dove-like satst brooding on the vast Abyss*
> *And mad'st it pregnant* . . .
> (I.19–22)

Here the perception of divine power carries a sense of its tenderness ("Dove-like satst brooding") within the encompassing sense of wonder and awe; the poet's mind, sure and confident, is utterly uncomplacent as it responds to what it is sensing as the *marvelous* creativity of God. Within ten lines we are hearing,

> *Who first seduc'd them to that foul revolt?*
> *Th' infernal Serpent; he it was, whose guile*
> *Stird up with Envy and Revenge, deceiv'd*
> *The Mother of Mankind* . . .
> (I.33–36)

It is our first image of Satan, as it will be our last. The quiet lines are full of rustling menace until, with the sudden rise in pitch and volume at "Stird up," we *see* Satanic malice, with terrifying power, actually rise up to tempt and to sting. Then the tautly coiled emotion gradually relaxes into "deceiv'd/The Mother of Mankind"; and the tender pitifulness of that, too, seems wonderful to the poet's mind.

The Father's is the slowest and the quietest voice in the poem. His first speech (III.80–134), though it often offends readers as a wordy protestation by self-conscious and unamiable innocence, is meant to show almighty power tenderly contemplating what in pure love it has made; and Milton, as he watches, is responding with joyful, lowly amazement at the marvel of it all. Sound transfigures the sometimes unalluring prose materials of his theology. The long extension of the sentences; the familiar effect of each line pulling against the center of gravity somewhere within the next; above all, the fusion of imperturbably slow pace with a slightness, even a tenuousness, of volume that yet makes itself heard: these devices produce an ordered continuum of sound which, like a violin bow or a singing voice prolonging a single note, increases the tension enormously. The Father almost never varies the tempo, and He never raises His voice. He never underscores a point; He does not need to. When we hear Adam say, in his final speech,

> . . . *by small*
> *Accomplishing great things, by things deemd weak*
> *Subverting worldly strong* . . .
> (XII.566–568)

we can understand exactly how that might be; in a sense, we have been hearing the thing performed in the Father's soft speeches all through the poem.

The Father does just what He is always saying He does: exalts the Son. That is both the doctrinal purpose and the actual poetic effect of His long speech beginning "O thou in Heav'n and Earth the only peace/Found out for mankind under wrauth"

(III.274–343). The tension starts to rise at once with the two opening sentences, seven and six lines respectively (274–286). Five short sentences follow. Then comes the massive sentence of twenty-five lines (305–329), eighth among twelve, most beautifully ordered into a three-part structure of eight, ten, and seven lines. "Because thou hast . . . and hast . . . because in thee . . .

> *Therefore thy Humiliation shall exalt*
> *With thee thy Manhood also to this Throne;*
> *Here shalt thou sit incarnate, here shalt Reign*
> *Both God and Man, Son both of God and Man,*
> *Anointed universal King, all Power*
> *I give thee, reign for ever, and assume*
> *Thy Merits; under thee as Head Supream*
> *Thrones, Princedoms, Powers, Dominions I reduce:*
> *All knees to thee shall bow, of them that bide*
> *In Heaven, or Earth, or under Earth in Hell . . .*
> (III.313–322)

"When thou . . . forthwith . . . and forthwith. . . ." This is Love perfectly loving Love Begotten, tremulously felt as such by the poet. Shorter sentences now sustain and increase the tension, on to the last, when — and not until when — we hear this ecstatic invitation:

> *. . . But all ye Gods,*
> *Adore him, who to compass all this dies,*
> *Adore the Son, and honour him as mee.*
> (III.341–343)

For it is an invitation more than it is a command; the appeal in the last clause, especially in the last word, is to love. It is not made until the scene's action of divine self-giving has been fully performed,[6] an action that has included something for the angels too: "reduce" (320) means "draw together." The Father is assuming that none of the angels can possibly miss the point, that Love is inviting a love which will increase their joy. Raphael later on, quoting the Father, projects the same impression: "him who disobeyes/Mee disobeyes" (V.611–612). If one gets the tempo and volume right, and the pitch, "Mee disobeyes" will sound not like a challenge but an invitation, which it is felt to be simply unimaginable that anybody could want to decline.[7]

The slow and very soft rhythms of the Father have precisely the effect Milton intends them to have, of projecting the Son into greatly magnified prominence and thereby of identifying Him as the Father's agent in external action. Milton has found a poetic way of doing something quite unprecedented, which can be sensed in all the Father's speeches but most obviously, perhaps, in Book VI. As the second day's battle approaches its noisy, violent end, all the good angels must be feeling that something has to be done, fast; and the verse works up to a fairly high level of excitement. Then we hear the Father speaking to reveal His will, privately to the Son (680–718). The speech is done in the Father's characteristic mode, slow, quiet, the emphases altogether unobvious. It suggests, of course, the divine imperturbability that we are familiar with, but now in a most striking way. The substance and manner of *this* speech, its particular substance and manner located at precisely *this* moment of the poem, suggest that there can be no need to hurry because the Father is outside time.

As soon as the effect has been caught one begins to realize that, in fact, all the Father's speeches throughout the poem are meant to sound the same way, as if they were coming from very far back, or very far within, from a plane and a mode absolutely unique. Milton thus seems to have discovered how to make sound enact the transcendence of the One.[8] The quietness, sometimes almost the whisper, of the Father's speeches is the very opposite of lassitude. It is a tenseness generated from the containment of tremendous energy, a sense of power held in that quite wonderfully suggests the tender, deliberate, and necessary self-restraint of infinite power as it deals with the frail creatures it has brought into existence. At this point in a discussion we always pause to bow toward Dante's superior tact. Yet Milton is not unaware of the problems he invited when he decided to make the Infinite a speaking character, and one can hardly wish he had decided otherwise, the result is so extraordinary. Our poetry contains just nothing else like it at all.

II

The flexibility and variety of Milton's responsiveness in *Paradise Lost* have not always received their full due. For one thing, comic notes, though decorously subordinated always to more grand and epic concerns, are often firmly registered. There is a pervasive delight in puns and other forms of verbal wit, as critics have recently been noticing. There is awareness, grim and sardonic and contained in fear, yet still genuine awareness of comic inflation in the characters of Hell. There is an attitude childlike and playful — and wistful — toward the antics of Adam and Eve's domestic zoo; in the last book there is a sense of mild and benevolent amusement at Adam's impulsiveness. There is even a sense for the comically enigmatic in the representation of the good angels looking at the new cannon, which Raphael so painstakingly describes — something of the impulse to chuckle that we manage to suppress as we watch a naive but clever child try to puzzle out a suspicious situation.

There is also a rich and continuous responsiveness to the physical world, to the enormous bliss of nature's abundance, and more particularly, to sensations of muscular action and of light and taste ("bright" and "delicious" are very potent words). But the joyous feeling for the world of nature, a sense so largely and variously physical, is also largely a delight in nature as the creation of God. For supremely, Milton's sensibility is moral and religious.

Yet it is not exactly that of a man at ease in Zion. Milton is feeling amazement rather; and joy which, though it all but overwhelms, is at last contained and shaped; and awe — amazement and joy and awe to find that any mortal creature should be invited into bliss. There is also tenderness, the sense even of a divine tenderness toward man, and a most intimately sympathetic tenderness of the poet's own for frail, threatened, sinning humanity. Tenderness and wonder, then, of a very special and complex quality, which is able to contain an appalled, unforgettable shudder that Satanic malice ever could be.

This epic arranges an endlessly interesting variety of modes for contemplating the wonders it is concerned with. Even the bad characters, in their way, seem marvelous to the poet, who is fascinated by their superhuman size and power, and awed by their bold malignity. The hoarse resentment against God that comes into Sin's voice as she is deciding to unlock the gate (II. 856–863) and the absolute selfishness of Satan's suave lines to Chaos and Night (II.968–987), a supreme instance of one person *using* another — within these dramatic enactments can be sensed the poet's amazement to behold such evil. Hell makes him tremble. For an imaginative realization of malignity pure and absolute, there is nothing in English to match Beelzebub's speech proposing the ruin of man (II.310–378); Iago and Edmund have scarcely a syllable to put beside it. Here the tense anticipation of a mind totally, hungrily, concentrated on destruction realizes itself in a quiet voice and, especially, a Satanic grin.[9] We have the same thing again, with the note of assurance and triumph added, in Sin's speech to Death as they set out to possess the Earth (X.603–609). Behind these, and every other such moment, there is a shudder at the malice of Hell, amazement at the thing itself, amazement that it could exist.

Milton's Poetic Art

The invocation at the beginning of Book III starts with an excited, exalted outburst which the sounds enact, "Hail *holy* Light, ofspring of *Heav'n* first-born," as of someone breathlessly emerging from darkness and suffocation. A sense of marvel lies behind everything, from the wondering speculations about light, to the tender sense of loss (intimate, but without self-pity), on to a sense of the more wonderful compensatory blessing of inward vision, to the petition, "that I may see and tell/Of things invisible to mortal sight" (54–55). It is a perfect preparation for the scene that follows, the divine will declaring itself as redemptive: another wonder, and felt as far more wonderful than anything yet seen. The book as a whole moves from the awed joy behind this first scene, through comic amazement at the foolishness of men to come, to the awed vision of the new created order still unspoiled. At this point everything that has gone before begins to fuse for us in a new complexity of attitude. A righteous angel and a sinful angel look at the perfect universe together (III.719–734); we observe them, and it, knowing that it too will be spoiled, knowing also that it will be redeemed.

Thereafter many varieties of wonder at the perfection of terrestrial order are enacted, never unmixed with a tender sense of pity for the frailty of man though still unfallen. The wonders that Raphael has to narrate come before us in yet another mode: heroic destruction and more heroic creation are both presented within the calm serenity of the perfect Garden, by a sinless angel to a sinless man invested with an awesome, racial, responsibility.[10] Then for a while, through emphases psychological and moral in Books IX and X, historical and theological in Book XI, it is mainly pity and fear that organize the poet's response to events, pity and fear as modes of the wonder which in complex elaboration is his total action. Book XII presents the scheme of redemption again, transposed now into the terms of historical narrative which is itself subordinated to Michael and Adam's epic interaction. The contemplation of this produces an amazed, wondering joy which, though it all but overwhelms, is finally mastered and then is incorporated with the tenderness in the lengthened perspective at the close.

The wonder and amazement continuously felt by the poet derive partly from his characters' wonder. Adam and Eve have many questions, about dreams and angels and astronomy and so on. They feel wonder, in the sense of curiosity to know; and when they get the knowledge they want, they feel the creation is even more wonderful than it seemed when they were puzzled. This is one way to answer the familiar charge that the life of innocence must have been a bore. That may or may not make good theological sense; the question is debatable. It is irrelevant to the literary criticism of *Paradise Lost* because it is simply not the response Milton actually makes to the prelapsarian life. His intense and eager interest can be kinesthetically sensed in the taut, alert muscularity of the verse as the narrator describes the Garden (IV.205–287; V.291–297). A different mode of the same response, equally alert but floated in more liquidity of sound, can be heard in the description of the moral life of the Garden (IV.288–324). It can also be heard in and behind Raphael's voice as he discourses on philosophy. "For know, whatever was created, needs/To be sustain'd and fed" (V.414–415), and even more clearly, "O *Adam*, one Almightie is, from whom/All things proceed" (V.469–470): these are not the impersonal formality of a lecture but the ardent glow of a mind suffused with joy in contemplating the truth it knows and marveling at it. Adam responds in kind (V.507–512, 544–548; VII.70–80). It is not just that he explicitly says he has been learning wonderful things. The fervency of his rhythms actually embodies his joy, as he discovers that the mysteries of the universe seem more marvelous when explained than they seemed when they were just mysteries, a state of mind that we can sense, for example, in the poise of these quiet lines:

> *What thanks sufficient, or what recompence*
> *Equal have I to render thee, Divine*
> *Hystorian, who thus largely hast allayd*
> *The thirst I had of knowledge, and voutsaf't*
> *This friendly condescention to relate*
> *Things else by me unsearchable, now heard*
> *With wonder, but delight, and, as is due,*
> *With glorie attributed to the high*
> *Creator . . .*
>
> (VIII.5–13)

The shock is therefore enormous when after more than eight books of a poem organized in this way we hear Satan begin the temptation, "Wonder not, sovran Mistress" (IX.532).

Extraordinary wonders of the physical order are made very prominent in Book XII, miraculous events in the order of nature viewed as subservient to the order of redemption: the Red Sea crossing, the stationary sun, the star of Bethlehem, the Incarnation, the virgin birth, the resurrection and ascension. Yet, however wonderful the order of nature may be, and the miraculous suspension of it, moral and religious truth and action are felt as more wonderful, by both the characters and the poet, before the fall and after it. That attitude is realized for the length of eighteen lines in the sound structure of a speech by Adam in Book VIII (180–197); and it achieves its supreme embodiment in the long last sentence of his final speech (XII.561–573), and in Michael's soaring response to that (575–587), each one exactly thirteen lines long, a fervent sense of wonder here at last consummately structured and controlled.

The responsive action sketched in these last few pages, frequently overt in the materials of the story, is dynamically continuous in the poetic mind that is contemplating and responding to the story. It does not involve the reconciliation of contrary impulses to any conspicuous degree; sympathies are consistently distributed throughout. But it is complex and it is coherent.

> . . . *What in me is dark*
> *Illumin, what is low raise and support;*
> *That to the highth of this great Argument*
> *I may assert Eternal Providence,*
> *And justifie the wayes of God to men.*
> (I.22–26)

— "and Providence thir guide" (XII.647). The end, so different from the beginning, yet recalls it; and thinking of them together, one sees what an expansive activity of mind it is that contains and links them. The action of sensibility that distinguishes *Paradise Lost* has at its center the enactment, thereby the discovering and ordering, of this spacious attitude.

Postscript

I

A few observations may be added here at the end, not as conclusions formally demonstrated but simply as generalizations about Milton's thought and art that have gradually clarified themselves with the writing of these essays. In the first section I should like occasionally to glance at *Paradise Regained* and *Samson Agonistes* as well as at the poems discussed in this volume, in order to suggest how the generalizations may apply also to those other two major works.

We may look first at matters of thought. Milton's religious faith is the most important thing in life to him, both as man and as artist.[1] Those aspects of his thought that have figured most prominently in these essays have consequently been certain religious ideas that keep recurring throughout his career as implications of his works. They make a large contribution to the total coherence of each major poem because Milton thinks and feels his way to them in the process of writing; "the very critical art of composition"[2] itself helps to make them characteristic of the way he understands the Christian faith.

Most obvious is the theme of divine rescue. Milton typically chooses as his subject for a poem a situation in which a human being encounters some evil from which he cannot escape through his own unassisted powers. Sometimes the evil involves supernatural enemies (as in the Ludlow *Mask* and *Paradise Lost*), sometimes more or less natural calamities which the victim may or may not have brought upon himself (as in *Samson Agonistes* and *Lycidas*, respectively). Always the evil is complex, involving both moral and physical dimensions, though the predominant mode of affliction may shift from moment to moment. But even the physical evils (premature death by violence in *Lycidas*, slavery and blindness in *Samson Agonistes*) are always perceived in a moral and religious context which shows that if in any way the protagonist is to transcend them, he must do so by being rescued. Divine grace is seen as ultimately the only answer for whatever evils man may suffer; and Christianity itself is understood as, very precisely, the religion of a *Saviour*.

The exception that rather neatly proves the rule is *Paradise Regained*. Although certain elements of divine rescue are involved in the action,[3] the poem has for its chief character not an ordinary human being who needs rescue but the Rescuer himself. It is a poem about the testing of this hero, the God-Man who by his spiritual strength is able to repulse every attack of the enemy. Through his spiritual victory he achieves, and in that sense demonstrates, his readiness to begin the heroic rescue of mankind.

In *Lycidas*, *Paradise Lost*, and *Samson Agonistes*, Milton dramatizes actions involving characters who at some juncture in their experience are strongly tempted to believe that God is unjust. The discovery may come late, but it always does come, that He is not only just but merciful; that, in fact, divine Justice toward man is Mercy. From *Lycidas* to *Samson Agonistes*, each of Milton's plots eventuates in a resolution wherein more good has been received by the main character(s) than has been expected or even desired by them. Hence the feeling of surprise and wonder so prominent in all these works. This poet never stops feeling amazement before the fact that rescue is offered to man at all; and repeatedly as Milton contemplates the astonishing abundance of good that God brings out of evil in the process of rescuing this man or that, what develops through poem after poem is a sense of the divine generosity.

It is from the feeling of amazement which Milton always experiences in contemplating the action of God as Rescuer that much of the dramatic excitement in his works arises. In *Lycidas* the realization comes with startling suddenness at the turn (165), where the poet creatively exploits a traditional feature in the "plot" of elegy in order to give dramatic point and vividness to his insight. The element of dramatic surprise develops more gradually in *Paradise Lost*: how Adam learns about the divine act of rescue, how he responds with prolonged amazement and accepts for himself the offer of redemption, make up the dramatic story that Milton has to tell in the later books of the long epic. His brief epic, the gravely beautiful poem that Lewalski has recently done so much to illuminate, again presents a rather special variant. Here it is not any among the race of fallen men but the enemy who is discovering the strangeness of God's ways with men — the enemy, simultaneously with Jesus himself. For the Rescuer, in the process of learning his full identity, is learning how astonishingly far God has been willing to go in order to effect the rescue of mankind. Jesus and Satan make the same awesome discovery at the same climactic moment (IV.560–562); and the angels' song of praise that follows (596–635), though naturally expressing no surprise at Jesus' triumph over Satan, does reflect their tremulous sense of wonder, and the poet's, as they contemplate the meaning of his victory.

In *Samson Agonistes* the discovery of God's amazing ways with men lies at the very center of the hero's dramatic experience. When the play opens, he is feeling that he has been cast away, and justly, by God. Then during the early scene with his father he formulates a distinction which is hopeless as regards himself (460–471) but which begins to be reshaped in the direction of modest hope as Manoa picks it up immediately: God indeed will vindicate His name, "But for thee what shall be done?" (472–478). In reality these are one single act, not two; the process by which they are drawn together and their singleness made manifest to the characters and to us constitutes the central action of the play. Not only has God chosen Samson himself as the instrument for vindicating His own name, in fact He has never cast off Samson; and as the hero moves toward the first insight, he perceives the second also. His implicit recognition of the full truth shines forth in the growing poise, the firmness that develops in the rhythm of his last speeches (1381–1389, 1399–1409, 1413–1426). Manoa, too, perceives (1718–1724); and the Chorus, achieving its own insight into the astonishing nature of God's justice, makes the element of surprise quite explicit (1749–1750).

From *Lycidas* onward, all of Milton's protagonists move to a profound sense of joy and gratitude by discovering how God deals with men. So, consistently, does the poet himself as he enacts his own response to the experiences that successively he dramatizes. Plainly, though, certain humbling implications are also involved for his conception of human nature. Man is intended to exercise the dignity of rational choice, his choices are real, and they have consequences that endure forever. Under God, man is lord of creation; but it is still God's creation, and He remains the supreme disposer of all things without exception, especially whenever evil must be dealt with. If evil is ever conquered in any situation, God alone wins the victory. Man has to trust Him for that, and indeed for everything, being called to respond in faith to whatever situation the Supreme Lord prepares for him, or permits. The nature of creaturehood itself as Milton understands it makes humble obedience the proper human attitude before God. Inevitably, therefore, man occupies a secondary place.

Not in spite of this fact but precisely because of it, Milton believes, man is a creature of very high status indeed. Voluntarily accepting the humble limitations appropriate to creaturehood makes it possible to reach, is indeed the necessary condition for reaching, the full stature of one's humanity. Such is the paradox that Milton dramatizes, repeatedly and characteristically. His redefinition of heroism itself has as its base this insistence, that in the nature of things man must willingly accept second place. Milton emphatically does not believe that man took a step

forward when he moved from original innocence to experience
through the knowledge of good and evil. Adam at the end of
Paradise Lost is a smaller figure than he had been in Books IV–
VIII. On the other hand, he is nobler at the last than he had
been in Book X. The evidence is the maturity and poise of his
final speech (XII.553–573), and the reason it has such dignity
is that Adam by grace is there accepting the grace of regeneration. Samson's rise to heroic stature comes about similarly,
through his receiving and then consciously discovering the divine favor, and his consequent act of accepting the divine will
for himself.[4]

Although naturally the short works of Milton's earlier maturity are less weighty in regard to this point, essentially they
involve the same stance. By the time *Lycidas* comes to its end,
the speaker has rediscovered the generous justice of God, and
by aligning himself with it has risen to poised, courageous acceptance of the human situation. Even the relatively simple
Ludlow *Mask* eventuates in triumphant dance, which is made
possible by the children's faultless love for the Good. One may
feel that understanding of evil is mainly external in this work.
However, the love which in the *Mask* is the poet's response to
Virtue has been profoundly experienced from within. The very
thought of Virtue enchants him, as the beloved enchants a
lover; and this genuine experience of love is what gives to the
Mask not only its fresh youthfulness but maturity and depth as
well.

The ideas and attitudes sketched in the preceding paragraphs form a part of Milton's general body of thought about
the great themes of nature, reason, virtue, freedom, and justice,
and the relation of divine grace to each. They help to make up
what is in its totality an attractive and vigorous creed, with
bone and muscle to it. Though all its essentials are familiar to
us in the general tradition of Christian humanism, the emphases

in the particular shape that has been described here belong to
Milton himself, serving as they do to furnish some of the
specifically Christian notes in the configuration that he individ-
ually gives to ideas and beliefs he shares with many generations
of thoughtful men.[5] Apparently it was through his art as a
poet that he found his way to his creed in the most winsome
shape he was able to give it. The controversial prose writings,
for all their power of mind, often seem ungracious; and the
scholastic formalism of the *De Doctrina Christiana* does not
allure. With the poetry the situation is totally different. As
A. S. P. Woodhouse wrote,

. . . for Milton the abeyance of his aesthetic sense always
means some impairment of his thinking. He is so truly a poet
that nearly all his best thinking is done in his poetry.

This is strikingly illustrated in his thought about religion.
Between the *De Doctrina Christiana* and the three last poems
there is no significant deviation in doctrine. But there is marked
difference in purpose and a wide disparity in tone. . . . the
De Doctrina Christiana fails precisely where the last poems, and
especially *Paradise Lost,* succeed. It fails because it is mere rational theology and neither religion nor poetry; and it was not
religion (one might almost say) because it was not poetry, which
from the first had been the principal medium of whatever there
was in Milton of genuine religious experience. Indeed, wher-
ever you take it, poetry seems to add as it were another dimension to Milton's thought.[6]

The preceding essays, although not stimulated by this comment, may be thought to illustrate it; and the ideas I have just
been sketching help to constitute the more or less doctrinal
bases for the emotional substance of the poems. They come to
us *through* the poems, as Milton himself reaches them in their
peculiarly Miltonic ambience through the art of poetry. That
is the point. The simple, sensuous, and passionate art that serves
him as his instrument to think with characteristically opens to

Postscript

Milton an organic experience of literary creation in which thought and feeling are indivisibly one. God, he believes, has instilled into him "a vehement love of the beautiful."[7] For Milton, to make a poem invariably means to perceive anew the "human face divine" (*P.L.* III.44) and "the bright countenance of truth,"[8] "Vertue in her shape how lovly" (*P.L.* IV.848), and — to sum up all — "hanc τοῦ χαλοῦ ἰδέαν, veluti pulcherrimam quandam imaginem, per omnes rerum formas & facies: (πολλαὶ γὰρ μορφαὶ τῶν Δαιμονίων). . . ."[9]

II

Repeatedly during the course of my study for this group of essays, I have found myself remembering a well-known sentence by Coleridge. "The poet, described in *ideal* perfection, brings the whole soul of man into activity, with the subordination of its faculties to each other, according to their relative worth and dignity. He diffuses a tone and spirit of unity, that blends, and (as it were) *fuses*, each into each, by that synthetic and magical power, to which we have exclusively appropriated the name of imagination."[10] With this famous statement in mind, I should like to make two observations about the characteristic working of Milton's poetic imagination.[11]

The first (which has not been very much exemplified in these pages) concerns his way of using literary allusions. Not always, of course, but very often when he echoes a phrase or idea in some text, Milton is remembering not only the detail itself but also its whole context. Of such a habit of mind two good instances that have been mentioned in the preceding essays would be the Scriptural echoes at the beginning of, respectively, the Ludlow *Mask* and *Lycidas*.[12] A few more examples may be offered here.

Doctrinal and artistic echoes of certain details in Ezekiel which occur early in *Paradise Lost* XI (3–5, 128–130, 377–380) have more than merely local reference. They may serve to re-mind us that in his total conception for XI–XII Milton is re-membering the whole book of Ezekiel, which is about the wrath of God and the destruction it will visit upon sinful men, with occasional forecasts of mercy and at the end the specifications for the new temple to be rebuilt by the remnant God will save.[13] Also throughout the last two books but especially in XII, Mil-ton is remembering Aeneas' visit to Hades; and again the total effect is wonderfully enriched by the range and discrimination of the poet's awareness. He is concentrating more consistently than Virgil on a particular line of descendants as it comes to focus in one very special Person. He thinks it worth remember-ing, also, that the two protagonists are being conducted to very different places by different kinds of supernatural guides, and that his episode differs from Virgil's in emotional tonality and movement. For Milton sees in Adam's great descendant the real and true fulfillment of what Virgil thought he saw realized in Augustus:

> "Quin et avo comitem sese Mavortius addet
> Romulus, Assaraci quem sanguinis Ilia mater
> educet. viden, ut geminae stant vertice cristae
> et pater ipse suo superum iam signat honore?
> en huius, nate, auspiciis illa incluta Roma
> imperium terris, animos aequabit Olympo . . ."
> (VI.777–782) [14]

Rolfe Humphries' translation strikingly recalls Milton's poem at XII.368–372:

> "And there will be a son of Mars; his mother
> Is Ilia, and his name is Romulus,
> Assaracus' descendant. On his helmet
> See, even now, twin plumes; his father's honor
> Confers distinction on him for the world.
> Under his auspices Rome, that glorious city,
> Will bound her power by earth, her pride by heaven . . ." [15]

Postscript

Verbal echoes too are likely to be more than simply verbal. When Adam overconfidently tells Eve that "the bitterness of death/Is past, and we shall live" (XI.157–158), we might predict the speed with which a desolating correction will be administered. Milton is remembering Agag speaking to Samuel: "Surely the bitterness of death is past. And Samuel said, As thy sword hath made women childless, so shall thy mother be childless among women. And Samuel hewed Agag in pieces before the Lord in Gilgal" (1 Sam. xv.32–33). We may feel therefore a second, special, level of irony in Adam's next words: "Whence Haile to thee,/*Eve* rightly call'd, Mother of all Mankind" (158–159).

Again, we can define Adam's situation with a new fullness and precision when we see that he has in him something of both Macbeth and Macduff, and when at the same time we are reminded of Exeter's description of two deaths in battle. After the vision of diseases Adam

> . . . *wept,*
> *Though not of Woman born; compassion quell'd*
> *His best of Man, and gave him up to tears*
> *A space . . .*
>   (XI.495–498)

The three passages here echoed are the following:

> *Accursed be that tongue that tells me so,*
> *For it hath cow'd my better part of man!*
>   (Macbeth V.viii.17–18)

> *Though Birnam Wood be come to Dunsinane,*
> *And thou oppos'd, being of no woman born . . .*
>   (Macbeth V.viii.30–31)

> *And so, espous'd to death, with blood he seal'd*
> *A testament of noble-ending love.*
> *The pretty and sweet manner of it forc'd*
> *Those waters from me which I would have stopp'd;*

> *But I had not so much of man in me,*
> *And all my mother came into mine eyes*
> *And gave me up to tears.*
>   (*Henry V* IV.vi.26–32) [16]

The fusion of Shakespearean echoes, impressive enough just verbally, is far more than verbal; and the whole passage, marking as it does one stage in the extended action by which Adam learns about death, is crowned by the brilliant transmutation of "cow'd" into "quell'd," placed emphatically at the end of a line.[17] Later again, in Book XII, when Adam exclaims after an early part of Michael's narrative, "now I see/His day, in whom all Nations shall be blest" (276–277), we perceive the irony in his mistaking Abraham's day for Christ's, and we feel a special emphasis on Adam's eager excitement when we remember that the echo here comes from an anecdote about an attempt by hostile and unbelieving people to discover Jesus' true identity (John viii.56).

All these instances of a notably characteristic gesture of Milton's mind may suggest a useful principle. Once an allusion has been recognized, it is always worthwhile to remember the context of the allusion in the work being echoed. Frequently in this way, one's perception and enjoyment of the artistic effect Milton is aiming at will be greatly enriched.[18]

The second general observation has been more frequently exemplified in these essays. One recurring implication has been the extraordinary measure of imaginative unity into which, for any given poem, Milton is able to fuse many varied materials. This power realizes itself simultaneously at every level, and in the relation between the levels, of plot, characterization, thought, and diction.

Some of the most striking instances of "that synthetic and magical power" at work in Milton's poems are matters of organic relations among a mass of local details. *Lycidas* has an astonishing homogeneity of imaginative texture; even the materials that have often been considered most heterogeneous, and therefore not strictly appropriate to the pastoral mode, can be shown to have been assimilated into the general body congruously with the requirements of genre and theme. The great long epic, too, may exemplify in its smallest verbal details the working of a powerful artistic imagination. Consider, for example, the complex activity of mind involved in the opening lines of Book XI, where Milton has the narrator move from the abstract, highly technical reference to a doctrine of theology ("Prevenient Grace" — 3), to a metaphor ("The stonie from thir hearts" — 4) that he has learned from Ezekiel xi.19 and xxxvi.26 (and already used at III.189), which consequently suggests for lines 5–8 an echo from Romans viii.26 ("the Spirit itself maketh intercession for us"). This last, in turn, brings to mind another verse in the same chapter of Romans ("For ye have not received the spirit of bondage again to fear; but ye have received the Spirit of adoption, whereby we cry, Abba, Father" — v. 15), which perhaps suggests the idea in lines 8–9, to express which Milton admits a pun ("yet thir port/Not of mean suiters, nor important less/Seem'd thir Petition"), by which he arrives at the classical analogue to the story of Noah (with which Book XI is going to end).

This is a good example of a procedure that John Ciardi, with his eye on a passage in Book IX, has spoken of as "A Poem Talks to Itself: One Thing Calls Another Into Being." [19] The process is going on everywhere in Milton's poetry, the continuous action of an imagination delicately alert to perceive links of many kinds. All the furnishings of his mind seem always on call. An extraordinary instance, involving a creative transmutation of materials, occurs late in *Paradise Lost* XI, in the lines about Noah here printed without italics:

Milton's Poetic Art

. . . hee oft
Frequented thir Assemblies, whereso met,
Triumphs or Festivals, and to them preachd
Conversion and Repentance, as to Souls
In Prison under Judgements imminent:
But all in vain . . .

(721–726)

In 1 Peter iii.19, Christ is said to have "preached unto the spirits in prison," and v. 20 refers to Noah, the ark, and the disobedient, identifying the latter as the imprisoned spirits to whom Christ preached. From the three verses, 19–21, were developed both the idea of the harrowing of hell and the familiar typological pattern, water as a type of baptism, the ark as a type of the church, and Noah as a type of Christ. Milton in a sense reverses the latter, and foreshortens the view of "the spirits in prison" — an imaginative transformation not totally unlike T. S. Eliot's superb re-creation, "I had not thought death had undone so many." [20]

The working of the same imaginative power may be observed from the larger perspective of architectonic plan. *Paradise Lost* is one solid whole. Even such blocks of "inset" material as the narrative of the war in Heaven and the prophecy of Biblical history have been imaginatively grafted into the total poetic structure. The Ludlow *Mask,* too, is all of a piece. A useful point may be made by reference to one of my errors as a graduate student, a mistake that comments instructively both about Milton's imagination and about another topic that has figured prominently in these essays, his fidelity to the principles of genre and decorum.

Like many other readers who have studied the *Mask* with enjoyment, I have believed that its plot was imperfectly adjusted to its theme, that the action of the drama did not cohere with the philosophy of the speeches. So my graduate thesis

134

included a statement about "unresolved complexities" in the *Mask* that "force us to look first from one point of view, then from another, and thus make impossible a single over-all view in which all the facets can be harmoniously fused." [21] The lesson is clear. I knew Milton's thinking about "most innocent nature," and I had perceived something of its relevance for the theme and action of his *Mask*. What I neglected was the essential nature of masque itself, which makes its own distinctive assumptions and which exists in a manner and for a purpose very different from those of drama for the stage. But if one goes to this *Mask* with the appropriate expectations, and takes also an understanding of relevant ideas in Milton's philosophy, all the difficulties vanish. Action, characterization, thought, and diction will all be seen to coalesce in a most appealing artistic unity.

If these essays can be said to have a single unifying logic, it goes somewhat as follows. For Milton, decorum is always the grand masterpiece to observe; he can therefore always be counted on to follow obediently the principles of genre; and he is able to follow them because almost invariably, no matter what goals his daring spirit may have chosen for a poem, his imagination is equal to the task of fusing whatever materials he admits. If we go to any poem by this artist assuming that he will respect the decorum of its genre, we shall be unfailingly rewarded; and we may possibly conclude that no poet in English has ever more amply fulfilled the terms of Coleridge's normative description.

Appendix

Lloyd E. Berry has published a manuscript version of Giles
Fletcher's poem *De Literis Antiquae Britanniae* which he dates
c. 1570–1571: "Five Latin Poems by Giles Fletcher, the Elder,"
Anglia, LXXIX (1962), 338–377. (The poem in question appears on pp. 345–363.) The short and undetailed passage about
Sabrina in the earlier version (only nine lines, 236–244) was
greatly expanded for the text that Phineas Fletcher published
at Cambridge in 1633. Since the later version is not easily accessible, I reproduce the relevant passage here, from a copy in
the Folger Shakespeare Library (pp. 5–6):

> At *Scythicâ* fessus glacie, *Rhodopéque* nivali
> Bella ferens, cladésque *Humber,* Nomadúmque phalanges,
> *Cambrum* acie, juvenémque ferox domat *Albanactum;*
> (Heu fortes nequicquam animas!) quos sanguine victor
> Mox *Scythico,* hostilíque piabat caede *Locrinus.*
> Ast Aquilis *Humber* pulsis, fractísque maniplis,
> Cedere paulatim, & lento vestigia gressu
> Ad fluvium (turgens irâ) improperata referre:
> Acriùs incumbunt *Britones,* turbántque, premúntque
> Ictibus: is tectus telísque undisque *Britanno*
> Infelix vitam, noménque reliquerat amni.
> Jámque etiam tumet, & Regali tardior *Humber*
> Incessu, nunquam placidis irascitur undis:
> *Marte* perit victus, *Neptunóque* obrutus *Humber.*
> At *Scythico* captus vultu, fletúque decoro,
> Captivam implorat victor; lacrymísque *Locrinus*
> Foemineis cessit, (madidis immersus ocellis)
> Mox exoravit, thalamíque in parte locavit.
> At miser implexae (miser, & suspensus amator)
> Fraude domus, saxóque tegens mala furta doloso,
> (Ah!) miseram illicito *Sabrinam* sustulit igne.
> Jámque decem virgo, septémque reliquerat annos
> Nubilis, uxori tandem cùm laesa patebant
> Foedera vesanae, & spreti perjuria lecti.
> Nec queritur, lugétve; acri furit, aestuat ira;
> Seráque corde viri pressans, animóque volutans
> Crimina, *Marte* fero mendacem, armísque virago
> Aggreditur Regem, quà plenus ditia culta
> Irrigat, & tumidâ *Severnus* volvitur undâ.

Ille acies bello fractas, captósque maniplos
Indignatus, atrox stricto sibi pectora ferro
(Foemineis bis jam domita armis pectora) rupit.
Regem fida comes pelléx (miserabile corpus)
Procubuit super, & tepidos misera induit enses.
At matris fato infelix exterrita virgo,
Dum fugit ultricis vultum *Sabrina* novercae,
Severni insistens ripis, ubi plena *Vitorgum*
Unda lavat; *Severne* pater, *Severne*, ciebat,
Cujus ego ripis solita olim, & flumine curvo
Ludere; si meritos tuleram tibi semper honores,
Si tua flore libens rapto, violísque, rosísque
Aequora, si lauro nexis, myrtóque coronis
Aspersi, miserere pater morientis, & istam
(Siqua via est) animam tristi defende novercae.
  Audiit, & miserans pallentem morte futurâ
Abstulit in vitreas sedes, ubi regia Nymphis
Jura dedit, thalamíque libens in honore locavit,
Dixit & immersâ *Sabrinam* à virgine flumen.

Then fierce Humber, waging war on snowy Rhodope and enduring the slaughter and phalanxes of the Nomads, being wearied by the Scythian ice, overcomes Camber with the sword, and the young Albanact (spirits brave in vain, alas!). Victorious Locrine soon avenged them with Scythian blood and with slaughter of the enemy. But Humber, swelling with anger, his standards beaten down and his troops shattered, gradually yields and with slow step retraces his lingering footsteps to the river. The Britons lay on more fiercely, and throw his troops into disorder, and pursue them with attacks. That unfortunate man, covered with spears and waves, gave up his life and left his name to a British river. And now still, Humber swells and, more sluggish than a regal pace, is never angry at its placid waves. Humber perishes, overcome by Mars and overwhelmed by Neptune. But the victor, himself captivated by the face and decorous weeping of a Scythian, entreats his captive. Locrine surrendered to female tears; and drowned in her dear weeping eyes, he soon prevailed upon her to share his bed. But the wretched man (a lover miserable and anxious), miserable because of the crime in which he had involved his house and hiding his wicked deceit with a stone cleverly placed, (Ah!) destroyed the wretched Sabrina with his illicit passion.

Now when this virgin was herself of marriageable age, having completed ten years and seven, this treasonous union and the injuries done to her scorned bed became known at last to the wife. She does not complain, or weep and wail; she rages, she grows hot with fierce anger; and, though tardily, she attacks him with the courage of a man. Turning over these crimes in her thoughts, the virago assaults the deceitful king with fierce war and with arms in that place where the full Severn waters the rich fields and rolls with its swelling wave. The violent man, angry when his army had been broken in war and his troops captured, with his drawn sword tore open his own breast (breast now twice overcome by womanish arms). His concubine, faithful companion, lay over the king (pitiful corpse) and, wretched woman, put on his lukewarm sword.

But the unhappy virgin Sabrina, terrified at the fate of her own mother and fleeing the sight of her vengeful stepmother, arrives at the banks of Severn where its full wave washes *Vitorgum*.[1] "Severn, father Severn," she began to cry, "on whose banks and in whose curved river I once used to play. If I always gave you well-deserved honors, if gladly I strewed your waters with the plucked flower, with violets and roses, with garlands woven of laurel and myrtle, have mercy, O father, upon me as I die, and (if there is any way) defend my life from my bitter stepmother."

He heard and, pitying her as she grew pale with approaching death, took her away to his own watery seat, where he gave royal commands to the nymphs and gladly gave her a position of honor in his house; and he called the river *Sabrina* after the drowned virgin.

Notes

"Most Innocent Nature"
and
Milton's Ludlow 'Mask'

1. Stephen Orgel, *The Jonsonian Masque* (Cambridge, Mass., 1965), pp. 6–7.

2. Cf. *L'Allegro*, 117–130. In this essay and in those that follow, Milton's works are quoted from the Columbia edition: *The Works of John Milton*, ed. Frank Allen Patterson et al., 18 vols. (New York: Columbia University Press, 1931–1938). Hereafter referred to as *Works*.

3. The ideas have been discussed in my unpublished dissertation (Harvard, 1953), "Milton's Philosophical View of Nature." A few key texts may be noted here. Two phrases from *Tetrachordon*: "most innocent lesson of nature" (*Works*, IV, 117), "immutable nature" (p. 176). Five from *The Doctrine and Discipline of Divorce*: "the guiltles instinct of nature" (*Works*, III, 500), "the radical and innocent affections of nature" (p. 499), "blameles nature" (p. 511), "the faultles innocence of nature" (p. 397), "the faultles proprieties of nature" (p. 383). And a sentence from *Tetrachordon*: "The Gospel indeed tending ever to that which is perfetest, aim'd at the restorement of all things, as they were in the beginning" (*Works*, IV, 171).

4. See n. 22 below.

5. Hence the absence of drama in the ordinary sense of "dramatic conflict"; cf. Orgel, pp. 16–17. There is, of course, a less restrictive meaning for "dramatic" that makes the word obviously appropriate for the Ludlow *Mask*. In a very favorable review of Orgel's book, Edward Partridge has commented that Jonson's "masques are not poems punctuated by songs and dances, but dramatic forms whose very life requires words, rhythm, and movement, all theatrically represented. The masque is drama in its choreographic, lyric, and verbal quintessence, with audience and masquers drawn into one ritual community." *MLQ*, XXVII (1966), 474.

6. And plausibly so. It is "natural" for the characters to make the references, given the Ovidian world they inhabit; and for the poet the references provide one among his numerous ways for keeping us mindful of the *Metamorphoses*. The transformations referred to above are narrated in the *Metamorphoses* as follows: Philomela, VI.438–674; Narcissus, III.339–510; Scylla, XIV.1–74; Callisto, II.401–541; Daphne, I.452–567.

7. For the story of Circe's magic potion, see *Metamorphoses* XIV.248–307. For Glaucus, see XIII.898–968; for Leucothea and Melicertes, IV.416–542.

8. Scholars have differed about the source of the Sabrina story, though most have agreed that it comes mainly from *The Faerie Queene*. "The soothest Shepherd that ere pip't on plains" (822) is surely Spenser, but Spenser has nothing about Sabrina's transformation into a goddess (*F.Q.* II.x.17–19). I believe that for Sabrina's story Milton is chiefly indebted to a Latin poem by Giles Fletcher the Elder which sketches the history of British learning and especially the founding of the colleges at Cambridge, and which Giles's son Phineas published in the year just preceding that of the Ludlow *Mask: De Literis Antiquae Britanniae* (see Appendix for the lines on Sabrina). The sympathy for Sabrina, the madness of Guendolen, the word *novercae* (which occurs twice; cf. *Mask* 829), and other details suggest that Leicester Bradner was correct in proposing this work as Milton's source: *Musae Anglicanae: A History of Anglo-Latin Poetry 1500–1925* (New York, 1940), p. 39. I conclude that when the Spirit remembers, "Som other means I have which may be us'd/Which once of *Meliboeus* old I learnt" (820–821), and then — after narrating Sabrina's metamorphosis — explicitly reaffirms, "And, as the old Swain said, she can unlock/ The clasping charm, and thaw the numming spell" (851–852), Milton is thinking of Spenser as his source not for the story of the goddess's transformation but for the interpretation of her moral nature and function. She does for the Lady what even Britomart cannot do herself for Amoret. And if the Lady is, in a sense, Amoret, she is the daughter of the Sun (like Circe), she has been adopted by Venus, and she has been brought up by Psyche in the Celestial Paradise (*F.Q.* III.vi.51–52). Hence one special mode of relevance — in a type of entertainment that exists to instruct by means of compliment — for the lines in the Epilogue about Cupid and Psyche (1002–1010). For other hints from *The Faerie Queene* that Milton may also be remembering, see n. 33 below.

9. Cf. Isabel Gamble MacCaffrey, ed., *John Milton: Samson Agonistes and the Shorter Poems* (New York, 1966), p. xxiv. Two recent articles also give some attention to the idea of metamorphosis in the Ludlow *Mask*: Roger B. Wilkenfeld, "The Seat at the Center: An Interpretation of *Comus*," *ELH*, XXXIII (1966), 170–197; Richard Neuse, "Metamorphosis and Symbolic Action in *Comus*," *ELH*, XXXIV (1967), 49–64. Not all of Neuse's instances are valid. When the Attendant Spirit changes into Thyrsis, and back again for the Epilogue (pp. 54, 62), he does not undergo metamorphosis

in the same sense that Sabrina and Leucothea have been metamorphosed (pp. 55–56). Nor does the text justify our supposing that haemony has been metamorphosed (p. 53), or that the country dancers are "Comus' crew re-metamorphosed" (p. 59).

10. I take "this mortal change" (10) to mean "this mortal realm of change" — i.e., of changing being.

11. For a similar answer to the question, derived from assumptions similar to mine, see Rosemond Tuve, "Image, Form and Theme in *A Mask*," in *Images and Themes in Five Poems by Milton* (Cambridge, Mass., 1957), pp. 112–161; and C. L. Barber, "*A Mask Presented at Ludlow Castle:* The Masque as a Masque," in *The Lyric and Dramatic Milton,* ed. Joseph H. Summers (New York, 1965), pp. 35–63. In "The Seat at the Center: An Interpretation of *Comus,*" Roger B. Wilkenfeld has recently argued that the Ludlow *Mask*, being a true masque, turns on a "hinge" that he interprets as emblematic in nature, the emblem of the Lady seated immobilized in Comus' magic chair. See also a recent article by John G. Demaray which, on the basis of Lawes's experience in masque, associates the Ludlow *Mask* with other examples of the genre that were produced in the earlier 1630's: "Milton's *Comus:* The Sequel to a Masque of Circe," *HLQ,* XXIX (1966), 245–254. Eugene Haun has also identified the *Mask* as a masque, but by assigning it to an extra-Jonsonian class of works loosely called "masques" which, although not closely connected with the court, were important for the development of musical drama in England: "An Inquiry into the Genre of *Comus,*" in *Essays in Honor of Walter Clyde Curry* (Nashville, 1954), pp. 221–239. See, in addition, n. 16 below.

12. Cf. Orgel, pp. 102–103.

13. *The Poetical Works of John Milton,* ed. Helen Darbishire, 2 vols. (Oxford, 1952–1955), II, 336–340.

14. ffrom the heavens nowe J flye
and those happy Climes that lye
Where daye never shutts his eye
up in the broad field of the skye./
there I suck the liquid ayre
all amidst the gardens fayre
of Hesperus and his daughters three
that singe about the goulden tree./
there eternall summer dwells
and west wyndes with muskye winge
about the Cederne allyes flinge
Nard and Casias balmie smells

Iris there with humid bowe
waters the odorous bankes that blowe
fflowers of more mingled hew
then her purfld scarfe can shew
yellow, watchett, greene & blew
and drenches oft wth Manna dew
Beds of Hyacinth and Roses
where many a Cherub soft reposes./

(Harris Francis Fletcher, ed., *John Milton's Complete Poetical Works Reproduced in Photographic Facsimile*, 4 vols. [Urbana: University of Illinois Press, 1943–1948], I, 303).

15. amidst th Hesperian gardens, on whose bancks
bedew'd wth nectar, & celestiall songs
aeternall roses grow, & hyacinth
& fruits of golden rind, on whose faire tree
the scalie-harnest dragon ever keeps
his uninchanted eye, & round the verge
& sacred limits of this blisfull Isle
the jealous ocean that old river winds
his farre-extended armes till wth steepe fall
halfe his wast flood ye wide Atlantique fills
& halfe the slow unfadom'd Stygian poole
but soft I was not sent to court yor wonder
wth distant worlds, & strange removed clim[es]
yet thence I come and oft frō thence behold

(Works, I, 479–480).

16. On the other hand, not all of the materials Milton added were explicitly Christian. In the Epilogue there are new allusions to Venus and Adonis, and to Cupid and Psyche. Note, too, that in 995 ("And drenches with *Elysian* dew"), *"Elysian"* had been "Manna" in the Bridgewater MS. (see n. 14 above). For comment on a Christian item that was ultimately rejected but which appears in the Trinity MS., see Barber, "The Masque as a Masque," p. 49.

A. S. P. Woodhouse inaugurated a new era in studies of the Ludlow *Mask* when he published his article, "The Argument of Milton's *Comus*," *UTQ*, XI (1941), 46–71. Although he complicated his thesis unnecessarily, I believe (with an elaborate scheme that locates Temperance and Continence symbolically in the order of Nature, Virginity in the order of Grace, and Chastity in an area common to both orders), his definition of Milton's intellectual frame of reference gave us an indispensable key for understanding the *Mask*. It will be obvious that I am profoundly indebted to "The

Notes to Page 9

Argument of Milton's *Comus*" and to Woodhouse's later article (see the following paragraph).

In the next year Tillyard published "The Action of Comus" in *E&S*, XXVIII (1942), 22–37. A revised version of the essay, which takes account of Woodhouse's first article and of others published in the forties, appears in Tillyard's *Studies in Milton* (London, 1951), pp. 82–99. Most discussions of the *Mask* since 1941, in fact, have involved extensions of Woodhouse's thought or reactions against it. The process may be observed in the following sequence of essays: J. C. Maxwell, "The Pseudo-Problem of 'Comus,'" *Cambridge Journal*, I (1948), 376–380; Cleanth Brooks and John Edward Hardy, *Poems of Mr. John Milton: The 1645 Edition with Essays in Analysis* (New York, 1951), pp. 187–237; Don Cameron Allen, "Milton's 'Comus' as a Failure in Artistic Compromise," *ELH*, XVI (1949), 104–119, reprinted in *The Harmonious Vision: Studies in Milton's Poetry* (Baltimore, 1954), pp. 24–40; A. S. P. Woodhouse, "*Comus* Once More," *UTQ*, XIX (1950), 218–223; Robert Martin Adams, "Reading *Comus*," *MP*, LI (1953), 18–32, reprinted in *Ikon: John Milton and the Modern Critics* (Ithaca, 1955), pp. 1–34; A. E. Dyson, "The Interpretation of *Comus*," *E&S*, VIII (1955), 89–114; and the essays by Tuve (1957) and Barber (1965) referred to in n. 11 above. Two other brief statements from Woodhouse about the *Mask* should also be mentioned: *Milton the Poet* (Toronto, 1955), pp. 10–11, and *The Poet and His Faith: Religion and Poetry in England from Spenser to Eliot and Auden* (Chicago, 1965), pp. 96–100.

Meanwhile, a different line of interpretation has been developed by reference to Platonic and Neoplatonic thought as the appropriate frame of reference. There are three items by John Arthos: *On A Mask Presented at Ludlow-Castle, by John Milton* (Ann Arbor, 1954); "Milton, Ficino, and the *Charmides*," *SRen*, VI (1959), 261–274; "The Realms of Being in the Epilogue of *Comus*," *MLN*, LXXVI (1961), 321–324. See also Sears Jayne, "The Subject of Milton's Ludlow *Mask*," *PMLA*, LXXIV (1959), 533–543.

Two other areas of thought have recently been suggested for frames of reference. Gale H. Carrithers, Jr., emphasizing what he calls "the civic, or the communal" (p. 35), argues that the *Mask* dramatizes a movement toward community: "Milton's Ludlow *Mask*: From Chaos to Community," *ELH*, XXXIII (1966), 23–42. Richard Neuse, in "Metamorphosis and Symbolic Action in *Comus*," sees the *Mask* in certain categories derived from psychology; see also n. 23 below.

17. Cf. Orgel, p. 169.

18. The restoration — or addition — of this passage for the 1637 text makes a notable improvement dramatically. In the acting version of 1634 the Lady had said, toward the close of her first speech,

> J cannot hollowe to my brothers, but
> such noise as J can make to be heard fardest
> J'le venture, for my new enliv'n'd spiritts,
> prompt me, and they perhaps are not farr hence . . .
> (Fletcher, I, 311)

But nothing in the action has shown how or why her spirits have been "new enliv'n'd." The Trinity MS., and thereafter the printed versions, have the evocative lines about her frightened imaginings (204–208), and then the lines reporting her vision of Faith, Hope, and Chastity (212–214). The vision is what enlivens her spirits; having heard about that, we can believe the statement about her "new enliv'n'd spiritts."

19. Cf. Josef Pieper, *The Four Cardinal Virtues* (New York, 1965), pp. 154–155, 166–167.

20. These reflections may help to remind us of what has been called "by far the best of all introductions to *Comus* and to much of Milton's earlier poetry, his own account, in *An Apology for Smectymnuus* (1642), of the growth of his youthful ideal of chastity and the reading that fostered it": Douglas Bush, ed., *The Complete Poetical Works of John Milton* (Boston: Houghton Mifflin Co., 1965), p. 110. Having summarized there his experience with "the Laureat fraternity of Poets," Milton goes on to say that

> riper yeares, and the ceaselesse round of study and reading led me to the shady spaces of philosophy, but chiefly to the divine volumes of *Plato,* and his equall *Xenophon*. Where if I should tell ye what I learnt, of chastity and love, I meane that which is truly so, whose charming cup is only vertue which she bears in her hand to those who are worthy. The rest are cheated with a thick intoxicating potion which a certaine Sorceresse the abuser of loves name carries about; and how the first and chiefest office of love, begins and ends in the soule, producing those happy twins of her divine generation knowledge and vertue, with such abstracted sublimities as these, it might be worth your listning, Readers, as I may one day hope to have ye in a still time, when there shall be no chiding . . . (*Works*, III, 305).

The Ludlow *Mask,* seen in the light of this passage, may be understood as dramatizing a story about the soul's true love. Comus's temptation into sensuous ease and pleasure is really an invitation to self-love ("Why should you be so cruel to your self . . . ?" — 678), which he represents as the ethic enjoined by Nature (705–754). Actually, his kind of self-love is not true *love* at all. Like his mother before him ("a certaine Sorceresse"), he is an "abuser of loves name" who tries to cheat the Lady "with a thick intoxicating potion." Or, in the language of the *Mask* itself, he is using "blear illusion" (155), the seductive eloquence that is one of his "dazling Spells" (154), to trick her rational will into accepting from his hand "this cordial Julep here" (671). So the question is, Which shall the soul love, itself or the Good? Rather, more philosophically, shall the soul "love" itself by giving itself to the pursuit of sensuous pleasure? Or shall it give itself in genuine love to the Good? For every soul will give itself to something. It is the nature of each so to do; and ultimately the objects that any soul can choose as the supreme *locus* of value for itself reduce themselves to two, its own self and the Supreme Good. The Lady can see, her purity of soul enables her to see, that these are in reality the terms of the choice she is being asked to make; "Vertue could see to do what vertue would/By her own radiant light . . ." (372–373. Cf. Pieper, *The Four Cardinal Virtues,* pp. 160–161). The choice each soul makes will determine what its ultimate destiny shall be, transformation into a monstrosity or into a god. In this way the quotation from Milton's *Apology,* invoked in the course of an effort to show that Chastity in the Lady is very much more than a merely negative virtue, brings us back to what was stated earlier in the present essay as the theme. The Ludlow *"Mask* is about the prospect of divinization open to all human beings who live virtuously" (p. 6); and love of the Good, which keeps the soul in purity, constitutes the dynamic for the life of virtue.

See also Douglas Bush, *English Literature in the Earlier Seventeenth Century, 1600–1660,* 2d ed. (Oxford, 1962), pp. 384–385; and William G. Madsen, "The Idea of Nature in Milton's Poetry" in *Three Studies in the Renaissance: Sidney, Jonson, Milton* (New Haven, 1958), pp. 206–208, 210–218. Also, cf. n. 30 below.

21. In this he may remind us less of the highly developed, philosophically refined, approach to theological discussion as perfected by St. Thomas than of the earlier, less precisely analytical, approach of St. Augustine. Cf. the illuminating statement by A. Gaudel, s.v. "Péché Originel," *Dictionnaire de théologie catholique,* XII (Paris: Librairie Letouzey et Ané, 1933), cols. 469–470:

Tandis que saint Augustin aimait à regarder la nature concrète et historique, telle qu'elle est sortie des mains de Dieu, comme la vraie nature, comme la nature normale, et tenait par conséquent ce qui est inférieur à la perfection primordiale, l'insubordination de la chair à l'esprit par exemple, comme un vice de la nature, saint Thomas va partir au contraire, la plupart du temps, dans ses analyses de la nature telle que la connaît la raison. Sa norme pour distinguer nature et grâce, ce que perd et ce que conserve l'homme après le péché, c'est la définition de ce que l'essence métaphysique de l'homme implique comme appartenant de droit à la nature. Ce n'est point que le philosophe oublie ici les données de la révélation: saint Thomas tient d'elle l'affirmation des privilèges de l'homme primitif; mais, pour caractériser ces privilèges, il conjugue les données de la révélation et de la raison: la claire vue des exigences de la nature pure l'aide à concevoir le caractère gratuit des éléments qui viennent surélever et perfectionner cette nature. Comme la nature humaine, considérée dans ses éléments essentiels et ses exigences, ne peut être touchée par le péché, avant comme après le péché originel, il existe dans l'homme un élément de bonté essentielle que rien n'entame: c'est la nature pure telle que Dieu aurait pu la créer. Voilà d'un seul coup clarifiée la distinction entre naturel et surnaturel, et limitées, d'une façon précise, les conséquences du péché originel.

Whereas St. Augustine loved to think that the true nature, the "normal" nature, was nature as it proceeded concretely and historically from the hands of God, and whereas consequently he understood whatever is inferior to that primordial perfection (insubordination of flesh to spirit, for example) as a defect of nature, St. Thomas on the contrary, most of the time, takes as the basis for his analyses nature as theoretically apprehended by the reason. His norm for distinguishing nature and grace, what man loses and what he retains after sin, is the definition of what the metaphysical essence of man implies as belonging by right to nature. It is not that the philosopher here forgets the truths of revelation (it is from revelation that St. Thomas receives the affirmation of the privileges of man in his first state); but, for the purpose of characterizing these privileges, he conjoins the truths of revelation and of reason. His clear view of the exigences of "pure nature" assists him to grasp the absolutely gratuitous character of those elements which come to raise and to perfect that nature. Since human nature, considered in its essential elements and its exigences, cannot be touched by sin (before as well as after original sin), there exists in man an element of essential good which nothing can harm: that inviolable element is nature, nature (metaphysically) "pure" as God could have created it. There we have the distinction between natural and supernatural clarified in one stroke, and simultaneously also the consequences of original sin precisely delimited.

See also the *Catholic Encyclopedia*, s.v. "Grace," "Justification," "Original Sin," and "Supernatural Order"; and for a historical study of the development of the philosophico-theological concept "supernatural," Henri De Lubac, *Surnaturel: Études Historiques* (Paris, 1946).

22. One thinks especially of *Il Penseroso*, Prolusion VII, *Arcades*, *Ad Patrem*, *On Time*, and *At a Solemn Music*. (The case for dating *Ad Patrem* as 1631–1632 has recently been restated and amplified by Douglas Bush, "The Date of Milton's *Ad Patrem*," *MP*, LXI [1964], 204–208.) George Williamson has discussed other ways by which the Ludlow *Mask* can be related to Milton's earlier works: "The Context of *Comus*," in *Milton and Others* (Chicago, 1965), pp. 26–41.

23. In his recent article, "Metamorphosis and Symbolic Action in *Comus*" (cf. n. 9 above), Richard Neuse expounds a very different meaning. Comus, he says, "represents a nature really disjoined from spirit" (p. 60); and "the Lady's encounter with Comus must . . . be seen from more than an intellectual perspective, as an encounter with the side of her nature below the threshold of rational consciousness . . . In the clash of sensual nature and chaste austerity . . . there comes about a paralysis. Sabrina's liberation of the Lady thus involves what is most profoundly natural in her, in that it is drawn up and presented to consciousness, as it were" (pp. 57–58). Neuse's interpretation, although it deflects the focus of the *Mask* into psychology and therefore away from the emphasis on morality that is Milton's chief concern, can hardly be proved to contradict anything explicitly said in the text. However, an idea stated earlier in the present essay may render unnecessary such a turn to psychology. If the Lady really "is an unfallen creature who sustains her position in an unfallen moral order that she calls natural" (p. 4), she is not vulnerable to the psychological disturbances

that Neuse's interpretation assumes. The suggestion that she is an unfallen creature has the advantage of probability on two counts: it is consonant with the general body of Milton's thought about Nature, and also with the character of masque as didactic compliment.

24. Cf. George Sandys's statement of an interpretative commonplace that he added for the edition of his *Ovid's Metamorphosis Englished, Mythologiz'd, and Represented in Figures* published just two years (London, 1632) before the Ludlow *Mask* was staged: ". . . *Circe* was said to bee the daughter of *Sol* and *Persis*, in that lust proceeds from heat and moisture, which naturally incites to luxury; and getting the dominion, deformes our soules with all bestial vices . . . which are not to bee resisted, but by the diuine assistance, Moly, the guift of *Mercury*, which signifies temperance" (p. 480).

25. Bush, ed., *The Complete Poetical Works*, p. 129, n. to line 638. Evidence for interpreting haemony as a symbol for divine grace has been presented by Edward S. Le Comte in "New Light on the 'Haemony' Passage in *Comus*," *PQ*, XXI (1942), 283–298. John M. Steadman has concluded that *knowledge* is the symbolic meaning for haemony, and has commented that Thyrsis' description of the plant is susceptible of a Christian interpretation: "Milton's *Haemony*: Etymology and Allegory," *PMLA*, LXXVII (1962), 200–207.

26. "Now the body is not for fornication, but for the Lord; and the Lord for the body" (1 Cor. vi.13. Quoted from the Authorized Version). Cf. Milton's use of this text in *An Apology for Smectymnuus* (*Works*, III, 306).

27. Cf. pp. 46–47.

28. Quoted from the version in the New English Bible (Oxford University Press and Cambridge University Press, 1961). And cf. 2 Cor. x.3–4.

29. *The Complete Poetical Works*, p. 129, n. to line 638.

30. This interpretation would be consonant with the *Mask's* own statement of its theme. Although the work is obviously about chastity and temperance (of which chastity is a mode), "virtue" is the only adequate single word for the theme; it is what we hear first (9–11), and also last (1017–1022). We may remember also that the term "virtue," though of course most familiar in the vocabulary of Greek and Roman moralists, does occur in the New Testament (Phil. iv.8; 2 Pet. i,3, 5). Now the passage from 2 Pet. brings "virtue" into association with "temperance" (v. 6: ἐγκράτειαν, "self-mastery"). 1 Cor. ix.25 associates temperance with an incorruptible

crown, and one of the standard cross-references for that text is James i.12: "Blessed is the man that endureth temptation: for when he is tried, he shall receive the crown of life, which the Lord hath promised to them that love him." (Cf. also 2 Tim. ii.5, iv.8; 1 Pet. v.4; Rev.ii.10.) By suggesting these texts, the Spirit's opening lines establish, permanently and from the start, a positive Christian dimension for the ethic affirmed by the *Mask*. Cf. n. 20 above.

31. For an echo of Eph. vi in a martial image, see the descriptions of Arthur's shield in *F.Q.* I.vii.33–36 and viii.19–20.

32. *The Complete Poetical Works*, p. 111.

33. Milton may be remembering, among other things, *F.Q.* II.ii.5–6 (the special grace associated with certain waters), III.xi.14 (the power of virtue), and such explicit affirmations of heaven's care for distressed virtue as II.viii.1–8 and III.viii.29ff. Also see n. 8 above.

34. Don Cameron Allen, "Milton's 'Comus' as a Failure in Artistic Compromise" (above, n. 16). Also cf. Thomas Wheeler, "Magic and Morality in *Comus*," in *Studies in Honor of John C. Hodges and Alwin Thaler*, ed. Richard B. Davis and John L. Lievsay (Knoxville, 1961), pp. 43–47.

Justice for Lycidas

1. William G. Madsen has observed that a number of comments on the flower passage are unsatisfactory because they do not account for its function as dramatic speech: "The Voice of Michael in *Lycidas*," *SEL*, III (1963), 2–4. A word on the subject may therefore be in order here.

The speaker has not felt that the great voices from beyond the temporal order have given any help, so he turns again to the natural world in one last desperate appeal — not for explanation now (he no longer expects a rational explanation) but for a little temporary ease, which he hopes to gain by looking at some of the beautiful things that grow in the world. As he quickly and honestly acknowledges, however, the created world in which they exist is the same order that contains the sounding seas; it is useless to expect either explanation or comfort from the natural world. And so, as his last hope collapses, he brings his complaint to its climax in that passage (156–162) "than which," T. S. Eliot wrote, "for the single effect of grandeur of sound, there is nothing finer in poetry": "A Note on the Verse of John Milton," *E&S*, XXI (1936), 39.

The paragraph above, as well as the approach in this essay generally, will indicate how firmly I agree that *Lycidas* is a dramatic lyric and is therefore best read as dramatic speech. See the whole of Madsen's article, and an essay to which he refers (p. 2), M. H. Abrams, "Five Types of *Lycidas*," in *Milton's Lycidas: The Tradition and the Poem*, ed. C. A. Patrides (New York: Holt, Rinehart and Winston, Inc., 1961), pp. 212–231. Lowry Nelson, Jr., has also emphasized the dramatic character of *Lycidas* in *Baroque Lyric Poetry* (New Haven, 1961), pp. 64–76, 138–152.

The recent edition by Scott Elledge brings together a variety of materials that illuminate the poem in its literary context: *Milton's "Lycidas" Edited to Serve as an Introduction to Criticism* (New York, 1966). A bibliography of critical discussions appears on pp. 321–325.

A number of widely known discussions of the poem are assembled in Patrides' anthology referred to above, *Milton's Lycidas: The Tradition and the Poem*: writings by James H. Hanford, Samuel Johnson, E. M. W. Tillyard, John Crowe Ransom, Paul Elmer More, Josephine Miles, David Daiches, Richard P. Adams, Wayne Shumaker, Cleanth Brooks and John Edward Hardy, F. T. Prince, Rosemond Tuve, Northrop Frye, and M. H. Abrams. An annotated reading list appears on pp. 237–246. Several other studies should also be mentioned here: Arthur Barker, "The Pattern of Milton's *Nativity Ode*," *UTQ*, X (1941), 167–181, which includes a brief but important passage on the structural pattern of *Lycidas* (pp. 170–172); Ruth Wallerstein, *Studies in Seventeenth-Century Poetic* (Madison, 1950), pp. 96–114; A. S. P. Woodhouse, "Milton's Pastoral Monodies," in *Studies in Honour of Gilbert Norwood*, ed. M. E. White (Toronto, 1952), pp. 261–278; Don Cameron Allen, "The Translation of the Myth: *The Epicedia and 'Lycidas,'*" in *The Harmonious Vision: Studies in Milton's Poetry* (Baltimore, 1954), pp. 41–70; Ants Oras, "Milton's Early Rhyme Schemes and the Structure of *Lycidas*," *MP*, LII (1954), 12–22; George Williamson, "The Obsequies for Edward King," in *Seventeenth Century Contexts* (Chicago, 1961), pp. 132–147; Jon S. Lawry, "'Eager Thought': Dialectic in *Lycidas*," *PMLA*, LXXVII (1962), 27–32; Isabel G. MacCaffrey, "*Lycidas*: The Poet in a Landscape," in *The Lyric and Dramatic Milton*, ed. Joseph H. Summers (New York, 1965), pp. 65–92.

An excellent article by B. Rajan, often similar in purport to my own, appeared in print after the present essay had been completed: "*Lycidas*: The Shattering of the Leaves," *SP*, LXIV (1967), 51–64.

2. By the end of St. Peter's speech the full range of the loss that Lycidas' death has involved has been canvassed, though we should note that the analysis has been presented not analytically but in an organically poetic mode that steadily enlarges the theme by continuously reassessing it. "Comes the blind *Fury* with th' abhorred shears,/And slits the thin spun life" (75–76), the speaker says to begin with, in an accusation that, while allowing for a divine mind in the conduct of human affairs, indicts it as purposeless. Although Phoebus immediately denies the charge, in the imagery of "those pure eyes,/And perfet witnes of all-judging *Jove*" (81–82), the speaker is soon accusing the powers that be, now unnamed (and we remember the relatively innocent "blind *Fury*"), of something worse, a positive malignity of purpose ("rigg'd with curses dark," 101). Then at the end of St. Peter's speech we hear the assertion of a purposefulness that righteously avenges evil; that strange word "engine" further suggests rational contrivance (see *OED*, s.v. "Engine," sb. 4), and thus modifies the feelings aroused earlier by "the blind *Fury* with th' abhorred shears." Meanwhile "the shearers feast" (117) has already made us feel differently about "th' abhorred shears"; and "the faithfull Herdmans art" (121) has softened the bitterness in "the homely slighted Shepherds trade" (65). The weary sense of futile repetitiveness in "Yet once more, O ye Laurels, and once more," and the numerous other suggestions

(in the opening lines) of unreadiness and of the repellent but unavoidable obligation to act, are modulated into the opposite feelings of "Stands ready to smite once, and smite no more" (131). (And of course the continuity in "no more" is renewed at 165 and 182.) Thus it is in no simply and analytically "successive" mode that the loss to poetry, learning, and religion is canvassed.

3. *English Literature in the Earlier Seventeenth Century, 1600–1660*, 2d ed. (Oxford: Oxford University Press, 1962), p. 386.

4. The interpretation of the speaker's character and situation that I have offered tends to find some confirmation in a suggestion by David S. Berkeley ("A Possible Biblical Allusion in 'Lycidas,' 1," *N&Q*, VIII [1961], 178), who proposes that the first three words of the poem are echoing Hebrews xii.26 ("Yet once more I shake not the earth only, but also heaven"), which is itself quoting Haggai ii.6 ("For thus saith the Lord of hosts; Yet once, it is a little while, and I will shake the heavens, and the earth, and the sea, and the dry land"). If so, we may hear in the opening a bitterly ironic recollection of a Biblical context that exhorts Christians "not to lose heart and grow faint" (xii.3 — New English Bible) but to persevere in the faith they have received, reminding them that discipline from "God the Judge of all" (v. 23) shows He is treating them as sons (vv. 5–11). And the quotation comes from an Old Testament book about the neglect of God's Temple, and God's blessing upon the children of Israel when they resume their care for it. It would appear, then, that from the very first line the poem is preparing for lines 64–84 and 108–131, and beginning that fusion of Christian and classical elements which has always been so powerfully felt in the later sections.

The question raised by the sudden shift at line 165 has been considered briefly, and differently, in the valuable essay by M. H. Abrams, "Five Types of *Lycidas*" (pp. 228–229; see n. 1 above). Abrams summarizes his interpretation as follows: "By extraordinary dramatic management, it is at this point of profoundest depression that the thought of Lycidas' body sinking to 'the bottom of the monstrous world' releases the full implication of St. Peter's speech, and we make the leap from nature to revelation, in the great lyric peripety . . ." (p. 229).

The question has also been discussed in Madsen's article referred to in n. 1 above, "The Voice of Michael in *Lycidas*," which helpfully reasserts some common-sense principles. Yet one may doubt the thesis that Michael is the speaker of the consolation, to an uncouth swain who understands only in part. Milton clearly identifies all the other speakers heard by the swain; why should we suppose he leaves us simply to infer that it is Michael who speaks *this* speech? Madsen himself suggests some uncertainty as to just where Michael's voice ceases (p. 6). Cf. also Madsen's comments in his more recent volume of selections: *Milton* (New York, 1964), pp. 13–14.

5. Regardless of what was said on p. 21 about the uncertainty of the classical world with respect to the soul's immortality, there is no reason — since it is the richly suggestive poetry of Milton that we are dealing with — why Phoebus' speech should not bring to our minds both classical and Christian meanings. (See also above, n. 4.) The statements in my text do not contradict Tuve's: "The question of Milton's pagan imagery in *Lycidas* here comes up in its first form, and we make the first answer to it, that such *terms* do not make images non-Christian . . . This does not deny the judgement that the unambiguously full statement of Christian consolation in Christian terms may shine out with a more splendid and luminous clarity, in Milton's own imagination and to us toward the end of the poem": *Images and Themes in Five Poems by Milton* (Cambridge, Mass., 1957), p. 76. Cf. Marjorie Hope Nicolson, *John Milton: A Reader's Guide to His Poetry* (New York, 1963), pp. 95–96 and n., p. 96.

6. "Dear" in 173 is the same word, from OE *déor,* that entered the poem in 6 ("sad occasion dear") with the meanings "hard," "grievous," "dire" (*OED* quotes line 6). Those impressions were softened, in Camus' line, with a word from a different root (*déore, díore*), "Ah; Who hath reft (quoth he) my dearest pledge?" (107). "Lock's," in 175, recalls "his Miter'd locks" in 112, whose suggestion of an immortal crown (1 Pet. v.4; cf. essay on St. Peter's Speech, n. 30) is reaffirmed in classical terms by the reference to "*Nectar* pure" (cf. *A Mask* 837). "Miter'd" has itself been prepared for by "his Bonnet sedge" (104). *OED* indicates (s.v. "Mitre") that the Authorized Version consistently uses "mitre" for the ceremonial turban of the Jewish high priest, "bonnet" for the headdress of the ordinary priests.

7. Both Rev. vii.17 and John xxi.16 use the same verb, ποιμαίνω, to shepherd.

8. See the essay, "The Decorum of St. Peter's Speech in *Lycidas.*"

9. Cf. E. M. W. Tillyard, *Poetry Direct and Oblique,* rev. ed. (London, 1945), p. 82.

10. Cf. *Arcades* 44–60, where the Genius of the Wood gives an elaborately detailed account of his actions as a kind of benevolent and never-sleeping woodland ἐπίσκοπος.

The Decorum of St. Peter's Speech in 'Lycidas'

1. Discussed in the essay, "Justice for Lycidas."

2. For a bibliography of articles and notes on the two-handed engine, see C. A. Patrides, ed., *Milton's Lycidas: The Tradition and the Poem* (New York, 1961), p. 241. Several more recent items may now be added to Patrides' list: Claud Adelbert Thompson, " 'That Two-Handed Engine' Will Smite: Time Will Have a Stop," *SP*, LIX (1962), 184–200; Byno R. Rhodes, "Milton's 'Two-Handed Engine,' " *N&Q*, XIII (1966), 24; Daniel Stempel, "John Knox and Milton's 'Two-Handed Engine,' " *ELN*, III (1966), 259–263; Ernest Tuveson, " 'The Pilot of the Galilean Lake,' " *JHI*, XXVII (1966), 447–458. A bibliography also appears in Scott Elledge, ed., *Milton's "Lycidas" Edited to Serve as an Introduction to Criticism* (New York, 1966), p. 297, conclusion of note to lines 130–131.

3. *Of Education* (*Works*, IV, 286). On the basis of what he understands as Milton's tone in using the term "master-piece," Thomas Kranidas has questioned the reading that is conventionally given to the sentence in *Of Education*: "Milton's 'Grand Master Peece,' " *AN&Q*, II (1963), 54–55. See also his recent book, *The Fierce Equation: A Study in Milton's Decorum* (The Hague, 1965), p. 96. Kranidas' book-length discussion of his large subject amply supports the application I make, here and elsewhere, of the principle of decorum for interpreting Milton's poetry; but I believe that he does not establish his particular point about the statement in *Of Education*.

4. With the parallelism of "after the manner of Egypt" in verses 24 and 26 the Authorized Version achieves a memorable poetic effect which a more recent translation sacrifices to make the shift in meaning more explicitly clear: "O my people, who dwell in Zion, be not afraid of the Assyrians when they smite with the rod and lift up their staff against you as the Egyptians did . . . And the Lord of hosts will wield against them a scourge, as when he smote Midian at the rock of Oreb; and his rod will be over the sea, and he will lift it as he did in Egypt." This passage is taken from the Revised Standard Version of the Bible and used by permission.

5. In the Authorized Version "rod" and "staff" are used more or less interchangeably to translate three Hebrew words: *maqqel* (rod, staff), *matteh* (bar, rod, staff, tribe), and *shebet* (reed, rod, sceptre, tribe). In Isaiah x, *shebet* in vv. 5, 15, and 24 is translated "rod"; *matteh* in vv. 5, 15, and 24 is translated "staff," "rod" in v. 26. In addition, *choter* (rod, shoot, twig) is twice rendered "rod(s)," and "staff" or "staves" is the rendering for several other

Hebrew words: *bad* (bar, branch, part, bough), *chets* (arrow, handle), *ets* (wood, tree, stalk, staff), *mashenah* (stay, support), *misheneth* (stay, support), *mot* (bar), *motah* (bar), *pelek* (staff, distaff, circuit). ῥάβδος (rod, staff, sceptre) is the usual New Testament word, rendered sometimes "rod(s)," sometimes "staff/ staves." ξύλον (wood, timber) is translated "staves." *Virga* is the commonest word in the Vulgate, which also employs *baculus*, somewhat less often, and in a very few instances *sceptrum, fuste, lignus,* and *firmamentum.* The Junius-Tremellius version employs *baculus* rather more often than *virga,* and also uses *scipio* and *tribus.*

Two useful brief articles on the Biblical rod may be cited: *Dictionary of the Bible,* ed. James Hastings, rev. ed. by Frederick C. Grant and H. H. Rowley (New York, 1963), p. 854; and Madeleine S. Miller and J. Lane Miller, *Harper's Bible Dictionary* (New York, 1952), pp. 619–620.

6. Surely a relevant association for a poem about a death by drowning.

7. Vulgate: "me consolata sunt."

8. With the thought expressed in the italicized words, cf. the following: "And concerning the tithe of the herd, or of the flock, even of whatsoever passeth under the rod, the tenth shall be holy unto the Lord" (Lev. xxvii.32); "In the cities of the mountains, in the cities of the vale, and in the cities of the south, and in the land of Benjamin, and in the places about Jerusalem, and in the cities of Judah, shall the flocks pass again under the hands of him that telleth them, saith the Lord" (Jer. xxxiii.13); "And I will cause you to pass under the rod, and I will bring you into the bond of the covenant: And I will purge out from among you the rebels, and them that transgress against me: I will bring them forth out of the country where they sojourn, and they shall not enter into the land of Israel: and ye shall know that I am the Lord" (Ezek. xx.37–38); "And as for you, O my flock, thus saith the Lord GOD; Behold, I judge between cattle and cattle, between the rams and the he goats" (Ezek. xxxiv.17).

9. In *Epitaphium Damonis* 23 ("ille, animas virgâ qui dividit aureâ"; in the translation by Charles Knapp, "he that with his golden wand parts the souls"— *Works,* I, 299), Milton is perhaps remembering Matt. xxv.32 again, with very different feelings from those in *Lycidas* 130.

In *Of Reformation in England* (1641) he makes use of the identity between the pastoral rod and the royal sceptre: "First constitute that which is right, and of it selfe it will discover, and rectify that which swervs, and easily remedy the pretended feare of having a *Pope* in every Parish, unlesse we call the zealous, and meek censure of the *Church*, a *Popedom*, which who so does let him advise how he can reject the Pastorly *Rod*, and Sheep-hooke of CHRIST, and those cords of love, and not feare to fall under the iron *Scepter* of his anger that will dash him to peeces like a Potsherd" (*Works*, III, 69). This sentence, in which he saw a reference to Psalm ii.7–9, led Tillyard to identify the two-handed engine as "the iron sceptre or rod of Christ's anger": *Milton* (London, 1930), p. 387.

These verses of Psalm ii are rendered as follows in the Authorized Version:

7 I will declare the decree: the Lord hath said unto me, Thou art my Son; this day have I begotten thee.
8 Ask of me, and I shall give thee the heathen for thine inheritance, and the uttermost parts of the earth for thy possession.
9 Thou shalt break them with a rod of iron; thou shalt dash them in pieces like a potter's vessel.

Although the fact can prove nothing with respect to the question of how to interpret *Lycidas* 130–131, it is interesting to note that at least by the time Milton had brought the text of *De Doctrina Christiana* to the state in which we read it, he was explicitly associating Ps. ii.9 with the Second Coming and the Last Judgment: Bk. I, ch. xv (*Works*, XV, 301). Cf. also Bk. I, ch. xxxiii (*Works*, XVI, 361), where again he quotes Ps. ii.9 (with v. 8), this time in a discussion of the Last Judgment that has begun two paragraphs earlier with several relevant quotations, Matt. xxv.32 among them (*Works*, XVI, 357).

10. *The Church of Our Fathers as Seen in St. Osmund's Rite for the Cathedral of Salisbury, with Dissertations on the Belief and Ritual in England Before and After the Coming of the Normans*, ed. G. W. Hart and W. H. Frere, 4 vols. (London: John Murray [Publishers] Ltd., 1905), II, 154–155. By the numerals in parentheses in the paragraph quoted above, Hart and Frere indicate page numbers (to Vol. II) in Rock's three-volume edition published in London in 1849.

11. "Huic autem, dum consecratur, datur baculus, ut ejus indicio subditam plebem vel regat, vel corrigat, vel infirmitates infirmorum sustineat." *De Ecclesiasticis Officiis*, II, v, in J. P. Migne, ed., *Patrologiae Latinae*, LXXXIII, cols. 783–784.

When he is consecrated, a staff is given to him in order that he may rule the people subject to its sign, or chasten them, or check the weaknesses of the faint-hearted.

12. *"Baculus* ex auctoritate legis et Evangelii assumitur, qui et *virga pastoralis,* et *capuita,* et *ferula,* et *pedum* dicitur. Moyses quippe, dum oves pavit, virgam manu gestavit. Hanc ex praecepto Domini in Aegyptum pergens secum portavit, hostis signis per eam factis terruit, qui velut lupi oves Domini transgulabant. Gregem Domini de Aegypto per mare Rubrum hac virga, eduxit; pastum de coelo, potum de petra hac produxit, ad terram lac et mel fluentem, velut ad pascua hac virga induxit. Nihil autem haec virga fuit, quam baculus pastoralis, cum quo gregem utputa pastor minavit. Hic baculus apud auctores *pedum* vocatur, eo quod pedes animalium illo retineantur. Est enim lignum recurvum, quo pastores retrahunt pedes gregum." I, ccxvii (Migne, CLXXII, cols. 609–610).

The staff [*baculus*] is taken up out of the authority of the Law and the Gospel; it is also called the *virga pastoralis* [pastoral rod], the *capuita,* and the *ferula* [walking stick], and the *pedum* [sheep-hook]. Moses indeed, when he tended sheep, carried a rod in his hand. When he went into Egypt, he carried it with him by the command of God, and by wonders performed with it he terrified the enemies, who like wolves were devouring the sheep of God. With this rod he led God's flock out of Egypt through the Red Sea; with this he produced food from heaven and water from the rock; with this rod he led the people (as to a pasture) to a land flowing with milk and honey. Now this rod was nothing other than the pastoral staff, with which as a shepherd he drove his flock. This staff is called *pedum* [sheep-hook] by writers because with it the feet of animals are held fast. For its wood is bent into a hook in order that shepherds may hold back the feet of the flock.

13. "In Evangelio quoque Dominus apostolis praecepit ut in praedicatione nihil praeter virgam tollerent (*Marc.* VI; *Luc.* IX). Et quia episcopi pastores gregis Domini sunt, ut Moyses et apostoli fuerunt, ideo baculum in custodia praeferunt. Per baculum, quo infirmi sustentantur, auctoritas doctrinae designatur. Per virgam, qua improbi emundantur, potestas regiminis figuratur. *Baculum* ergo pontifices portant, ut infirmos in fide per doctrinam erigant; *virgam* bajulant, ut per potestatem inquietos corrigant; quae virga vel baculus est recurvus, ut aberrantes a grege docendo ad poenitentiam trahat; in extremo est acutus, ut rebelles excommunicando retrudat, haereticos velut lupos ab ovili Christi potestative exterreat." I, ccxviii (Migne, CLXXII, col. 610).

In the Gospel too the Lord gave command to his apostles that in preaching they should carry nothing except a staff (Mk. vi; Lk. ix). And since bishops are the shepherds of God's flock, as Moses and the apostles were, they likewise display a staff in their keeping. By the staff [*baculum*], with which the weak are sustained, the authority of teaching is signified. The power of governing is symbolized in the rod [*virgam*], by which the wicked are purified. Bishops therefore carry a staff [*baculum*] in order that by teaching they may encourage those who are weak in the faith; they carry a rod [*virgam*] in order that through its power they may correct the unruly. This rod or staff is curved in order that through teaching it may draw back to repentance those who stray from the flock. It is sharp at the end that it may thrust back the rebellious with excommunication or with its power may frighten the heretical (who are wolves, as it were) away from the sheepfold of Christ.

14. "Hic baculus ex osse et ligno efficitur, crystallina vel deaurata sphaerula conjunguntur, in supremo capite insignitur, in extremo ferro acuitur. Per baculum, ut dictum est, auctoritas doctrinae accipitur, qua grex Dominicus a pastore reficitur, et ad pascua vitae compellitur. Per durum os, duritia legis; per lignum, mansuetudo Evangelii insinuatur; per gemmam sphaerulae, divinitas Christi. Per supremum caput, regnum coelorum; per extremum ferrum, ultimum judicium denotatur. Ex osse ergo baculus inciditur, dum ex dura lege duritia peccantium reprimitur. Ex ligno tornatur, dum ex ligno vitae Christo doctrina formatur, et populus in virtutibus roboratur. Os ligno per gemmam connectitur, quia vetus lex novae per Christi divinitatem contexitur." I, ccxix (Migne, CLXXII, col. 610).

"Per sphaerulam enim dilectio intelligitur, qua severitas vel lenitas pontificis complectitur. Oportet enim ut doctrina episcopi ex utraque lege sic dilectione copuletur, ut Ecclesiam Christo conjungere per charitatem conetur. Haec autem cuncta sunt rasili arte polita; quia ista sunt omni sanctitate redimita. Os recurvatur, ut populus errans per doctrinam ad Dominum retrahatur. Caput in supremo ponitur, dum conversis vita aeterna proponitur. In extremo baculus ferro induratur, dum omnis praedicatio per ultimum judicium terminatur. In curvatura est scriptum: *Dum iratus fueris, misericordiae recordaberis* (*Habac.* III; *Tob.* III); ne ob culpam gregis superet ita [ira] mentem pastoris, sed verbo et exemplo revocet peccantes ad misericordiam Redemptoris. In sphaerula est scriptum, *homo quatenus se hominem memoretur*, ut de potestate collata non elevetur. Juxta ferrum est scriptum *Parce*, ut subjectis in disciplina parcat, quatenus ipse a summo pastore gratiam inveniat, unde et ferrum debet esse retusum, quia judicium sacerdotis per clementiam debet esse delibutum." I, ccxx (Migne, CLXXII, 610–611).

This staff is made out of bone and wood, which are joined together by means of a little sphere of crystal or gilt. At the top it is marked with a head; at the bottom it is pointed with iron. By the staff, as has been said, is received the authority of teaching, by which the shepherd nourishes the Lord's flock and leads them to the pasture of life. In the hard bone is symbolized the hardness of the Law; in the wood, the mildness of the Gospel; in the jewel of the sphere, the divinity of Christ. The head at the top signifies the kingdom of heaven; the iron at the bottom, the last judgment. Thus the staff is cut out of bone as the hardness of sinners is restrained by the hard Law. It is made of wood that has been smoothed with a lathe, just as doctrine is fashioned by Christ out of the tree of life and as the people are made strong in virtues. The bone is joined to the wood by a jewel because the old law is bound to the new through the divinity of Christ.

Through the sphere is understood love, which embraces both the severity and the mildness of a bishop. For it is proper that a bishop's teaching out of each law should be so joined with love, that he may endeavor through charity to unite the Church to Christ. Now all these things have been refined with polished art, because those things have been wreathed with all sanctity. The bone is curved in order that the people, if they stray, may be brought back to the Lord through teaching. The head is placed at the top while eternal life is offered to the converted. At the bottom the staff is made hard with iron while all preaching is ended with the last judgment. On the curve is written, "When you are angry, you will remember mercy" (Habac. iii; Tob. iii), in order that anger over the sins of the flock should not get the better of the shepherd's mind but that through word and deed he may recall sinners to the mercy of the Redeemer. On the sphere is written, "In so far as he is a man, let him remember that he is a man," in order that he should not feel puffed up by reason of the authority invested in him. Next to the iron is written, "Spare," that he himself may find grace from the Chief Shepherd as he is lenient to those committed to his discipline [lit., to those subjected in discipline]. Wherefore the iron ought to be blunted because a priest's judgments ought to be anointed with clemency.

A few other details may be found in two other twelfth-century writers. Hugo of St. Victor writes as follows in his *Speculum de*

Mysteriis Ecclesiae: "Baculus pastoralis rectitudine sui rectum regi-
men significat. Quod autem una pars curva est, altera acuta, mon-
strat praeesse subjectis et debellare rebelles. Unde dictum est:
  Curva trahit mites, pars pungit acuta rebelles.
Et iterum:
  Curva trahit quos virga regit, pars ultima pungit.
Et item:
  Attrahe per curvum, medio rege, punge per imum.
Et item: *Per baculum rectum doceas, episcope, recte vivere, per ferri
flexus properes misereri."* ch. vi (Migne, CLXXVII, col. 354).

The pastoral staff signifies right rule by its straightness. The fact
that one part is curved and the other sharp shows that he is in
command of his subjects and is vanquishing the rebellious. Whence
it is said:

*The curved part draws the gentle, the sharp part pierces the
  rebellious.*
And again:
*The curved part draws those whom the rod rules, the bottom part
  pierces them.*
And likewise:
*Draw in with the curve, rule with the middle, pierce with the
lowest part. And likewise: Through the straight rod, o bishop, may
you teach how to live justly; through the curvings of iron may you
be swift to have mercy.*

Robertus Paululus writes, in *De Caeremoniis, Sacramentis,
Officiis et Observationibus Ecclesiasticis:* "Huic dum regimen Ecclesiae committitur, baculus quasi pastori traditur. In quo tria notantur
quae significatione non carent. Haec sunt recurvitas, virga, cuspis.
Quorum significationem breviter aperit egregius ille versificator epis-
copus Cenomanensis versibus his:

  Collige, sustenta, stimula: vaga, morbida, lenta.
  Hoc est pastoris: hoc virga figurat honoris.
  Et iterum quidam dicit:
  Attraho peccantes, justos rego, pungo vagantes.
  Officio triplici servio pontifici."
    I, xl (Migne, CLXXVII, col. 401).

When the authority of ruling over the Church is committed
to him, a staff is given as to a shepherd. In this are noted three
things not lacking in significance. They are the crook, the rod,

the point, the meaning of which is tersely set forth by that distinguished poet, the Bishop of Cremona, in these verses:

Draw together, support, goad: the wandering, the ailing, the lagging.
This is a shepherd's task; the rod symbolizes this honorable work.
And likewise someone says:
I draw in the sinners, I govern the righteous, I prick the wanderers.
I serve the threefold pontifical office.

Discussions from the thirteenth century may be found in Sicardus, *Mitrale seu De Officiis Ecclesiasticis Summa*, II, v (Migne, CCXIII, 79–80), and at greater length in William Durandus, *Rationale divinorum officiorum*, III, xv. This standard work on ecclesiastical symbolism was often reprinted in the sixteenth century; T. H. Passmore has translated Book III: *The Sacred Vestments, An English Rendering of the Third Book of the 'Rationale Divinorum Officiorum' of Durandus, Bishop of Mende* (London, 1899).

Of the articles in various encyclopedias, the two most helpful are those in the *Catholic Encyclopedia* (s.v. "Crosier") and *Enciclopedia Cattolica* (s.v. "Pastorale").

Two recent discussions by Cyril E. Pocknee may be mentioned, both concerned with historical facts rather than with symbolism: *Liturgical Vesture: Its Origins and Development*, Alcuin Club Tracts XXX (London, 1960), pp. 44–49; "The Pastoral Staff or Crozier and the Primatial Cross," *Church Quarterly Review*, CLXVI (April–June 1965), 201–207.

J. S. P. Tatlock has commented on a bit of Chaucerian irony (an allusion to the crosier, in *Friar's Tale* 1317) in "The Date of the *Troilus*: and Minor Chauceriana," *MLN*, L (1935), 294–295. Skeat has a note on the same line, and refers also to *Piers Plowman* C, xi.92: *The Complete Works of Geoffrey Chaucer*, 7 vols. (Oxford, 1894–97), V, 323.

15. "Per virgam, qua improbi emundantur, potestas regiminis figuratur." *Gemma Animae*, I, ccxviii (Migne, CLXXII, col. 610).

The power of ruling is symbolized in the rod, by which the wicked are purified.

That the Biblical image of shepherd involves ideas of both nourishing a flock and ruling it may be suggested by the following texts: 2 Sam. v.2; 1 Chron. xi.2; Ps. xxviii.9 (AV "feed," Vulgate "rege"); Ps. lxxviii.71; Micah vii.14 (AV "Feed thy people with thy rod"); Isa. xl.11; John xxi.15–17; Acts xx.28 (ποιμαίνειν; AV "to feed the church of God"; Vulgate "regere Ecclesiam Dei"); 1 Pet. v.2; Rev. vii.17 (AV "shall feed," Vulgate "reget").

16. Durandus, III, xv, in Passmore, *The Sacred Vestments*, pp.

116–117. Some of the texts mentioned by Durandus in this quotation suggest that Milton may be remembering the phrase "rod of iron" when he represents one of St. Peter's keys as iron, and thereby refashions a symbol long familiar in Christian iconography. Usually both keys are gold, though sometimes (as in *Purgatorio* IX.118) one is gold and the other silver. Perhaps Milton imagines one key as iron by making connections among several texts in the Apocalypse: Jesus, who is to rule the nations "with a rod of iron" (ii.27, xii.5; cf. Ps. ii.9), is also described as having "the keys of hell and of death" (i.18); it is "he that hath the key of David, he that openeth, and no man shutteth; and shutteth, and no man openeth" (iii.7).

17. Certain features of the interpretation proposed in this essay for the two-handed engine have been anticipated by the following: E. M. W. Tillyard, *Milton* (London, 1930), p. 387; C. W. Brodribb, *TLS*, June 12, 1930, p. 496, and June 5, 1943, p. 271; Marian H. Studley, "'That Two-Handed Engine,'" *English Journal*, coll. ed., XXVI (1937), 148–151; Lowell W. Coolidge, "'That Two-Handed Engine,'" *PQ*, XXIX (1950), 444–445; Harry F. Robins, "Milton's 'Two-Handed Engine at the Door' and St. Matthew's Gospel," *RES*, V (1954), 25–36; E. L. Brooks, "'Lycidas' and Bible Pastoral," *N&Q*, III (1956), 67–68.

18. One secular medium for preserving knowledge of the symbolism would have been "that most clever *Praise of Folly*," which "is now in the hands of everyone," as Milton had said in 1628 (*Prolusion VI*, in *Works*, XII, 221). Erasmus has a paragraph that tersely summarizes the symbolism of all the insignia of a bishop, "most watchful care of the flock put under his charge" being the symbolism of the crosier: *The Praise of Folly by Desiderius Erasmus*, trans. Hoyt Hopewell Hudson (Princeton: Princeton University Press, 1941), p. 97.

19. Verse 24: ". . . he shall smite thee with a rod, and shall lift up his staff against thee . . ." But Milton would be likely to remember also that ῥάβδος itself comes from ῥαπίζω, which in the Authorized Version is rendered "smite/smote": Matt. v.39, xxvi.67; cf. John xix.3. Cf. also n. 42 below.

20. Verses 22–23, the thought of which is clearer in St. Paul's quotation: "For he will finish the work, and cut it short in righteousness: because a short work will the Lord make upon the earth" (Rom. ix.28). In editions of the Authorized Version of the sort that Milton used, Isaiah x.22–23 has a marginal reference to Romans ix.27–28.

21. For a rather different view, cf. the suggestive article by

Claud Adelbert Thompson, " 'That Two-Handed Engine' Will Smite: Time Will Have a Stop" (above, n. 2). Thompson affirms categorically his belief that the event referred to in lines 130–131 is the Last Judgment (p. 186).

The fact that the two epistles attributed to St. Peter, and notably the second, dwell so emphatically on the themes of the Second Advent and the Last Judgment probably helps to account for Milton's choice of this particular apostle as the character for this section of his poem. See esp. 1 Pet. iv.17–v.4; 2 Pet. ii.3–iii.18. If so, the point tends to confirm my thesis that the rod of Christ implied in Matt. xxv.32 is "that two-handed engine" of *Lycidas* 130. But even more important, I should suppose, for explaining why Peter specifically is the speaker Milton wants for lines 113–131 is the fact that it was "The Pilot of the *Galilean* lake" (109) who preached the first Christian sermon. Milton is remembering that when Jesus called Peter He promised to make the fisherman a fisher of men (Lk. v.1–11, Matt. iv.18–20, Mk. i.16–18), and that the result of Peter's sermon recorded in Acts ii.14–40 was to add to the Church "about three thousand souls" (v. 41). For comment about the emphasis on preaching in St. Peter's speech in *Lycidas*, see pp. 41 ff.

22. The irony derived from the relation between the crosier and Christ's rod seems to me typically Miltonic; the fierceness is Miltonic too. May this poet be remembering, in his own way, a phrase from *The Temple*, that winsome reflection in art of life within the Anglican obedience which had been published only four years earlier? Herbert calls prayer, among other things, an "Engine against th' Almightie" ("Prayer [1]," line 5); one sees the half-smile and hears the undertone of amusement, faintly but consciously present. The "engine" in *Lycidas* has nothing of that quality; the two images offer an instructive instance of the difference between the metaphysical manner and the Miltonic.

23. F. E. Brightman, ed., *The English Rite, Being a Synopsis of the Sources and Revisions of the Book of Common Prayer, with an Introduction and an Appendix,* 2 vols. (London: Evans Brothers Limited, 1915), II, 926.

24. *Ibid.,* II, 1014.

25. See p. 44.

26. *Convocation of Canterbury. Upper House. Report of the Sub-Committee appointed February, 1907, to draw up a historical memorandum on the Ornaments of the Church and its ministers* (London, 1908), p. 103. Hereafter referred to as *Canterbury Report.* Acknowledgment for permission to quote from this publica-

tion is hereby made to The Society for Promoting Christian Knowledge (S.P.C.K.).

27. Alcuin Club Collections, XXII (London, 1919).

28. Rev. ed. Vernon Staley (London, 1902–1904), Part III, plate facing p. 229.

29. One other interesting item may be noted. John Williams, Bishop of Lincoln (also Dean of Westminster, and in 1642 enthroned as Archbishop of York), although no Puritan, was not a Laudian either; but he seems to have used a staff. When in 1640, under the authority of the Long Parliament, he had been released from the Tower, whither some of Peter Heylyn's actions had helped to send him, he interrupted a sermon which that quarrelsome priest was delivering in the Abbey. As George Vernon tells it, four days after Heylyn "had received order to appear before the *Committee,* he preach'd his turn in the *Abbey* at *Westminster,* and in the midst of his Sermon was insufferably affronted by the Bishop of *Lincoln,* who knocking the Pulpit with his Staff, cried out aloud, *No more of that Point, No more of that Point,* Peter." *The Life Of the Learned and Reverend Dr Peter Heylyn, Chaplain to Charles I. & Charles II. Monarchs of Great Britain* (London, 1682), p. 109. The incident is noted in the *DNB* sketch of Heylyn's life.

30. Milton seems to be remembering the symbolism of the mitre as well as that of the pastoral staff. Duality is prominent in the whole passage. Two keys, two metals, two hands and, as Erasmus puts it, "the two-horned miter" which symbolizes "a perfect knowledge of the Old and New Testaments" (Hudson, p. 97). What seems to have dominated Milton's imagination in this context is the mitre's aspect of duality, which is the feature that made it possible for him to link "Miter'd" in line 112 with so many other items in the passage. For comment on links with other parts of the poem, see the essay, "Justice for Lycidas," n. 6.

In other aspects of its symbolism (suggested by such texts as 1 Cor., ix.25, 2 Tim. iv.8, James i.12, 1 Pet. v.4, Rev. ii.10) the mitre is seen as a protector of the five senses, a crown, and a helmet for use in spiritual warfare; cf. Durandus, III, xiii, in Passmore, *The Sacred Vestments,* pp. 94–98. When Milton is campaigning against prelacy in the 1640's, he occasionally sneers at mitres in a way that indicates his familiarity with their shape (e.g., *The Reason of Church Government,* in *Works,* III, 218) and with their symbolic meanings (*An Apology,* in *Works,* III, 366).

31. There is not much evidence about the character of Milton's churchmanship in his earlier years, and what does exist is not

easy to interpret. Elegy 4 raises a difficult problem. Douglas Bush
is surely right in detecting "incipient Puritanism" in it: *John Milton:
A Sketch of His Life and Writings* (New York, 1964), p. 30. In
that poem of 1627, Milton refers to Thomas Young as "Praesul"
(18) — strangely, since only a year earlier he had used the same
word with technical appropriateness in his poems commemorating
the deaths of two bishops (Elegy 3, title and lines 13, 53; "In
obitum Praesulis Eliensis," title and line 6), and the meanings
"bishop," "prelate," had been well established for the word in
medieval Latin: see J. H. Baxter and Charles Johnson, *Medieval
Latin Word-List from British and Irish Sources* (London, 1934),
s.v. *presul;* also *OED,* s.v. "presul." Of course, in applying the
trm *praesul* to Young, Milton may have meant no more than that,
for religious purposes, Young was the "presiding officer" for the
group of English merchants in Hamburg. Also, since *praesul* had
priestly associations in classical Latin, one may wonder whether it
was Milton's humanistic principles that were chiefly responsible
for his using it to refer, in Latin poems, both to the bishops and
to his old tutor (whose influence in stimulating his love for the
classics he especially celebrates in Elegy 4, lines 29–32). Cf. also
his use of *rex sacrorum,* another technical term from classical
religion ("In obitum Praesulis Eliensis," line 13); and see Douglas
Bush, ed., *The Complete Poetical Works of John Milton* (Boston,
1965), p. 21, n. to line 13. In any case, the application of *praesul*
within a year's time to Lancelot Andrewes, Nicholas Felton, and
Thomas Young is very odd; and it may strongly suggest that by
1627 Milton had perhaps already embraced the Puritan doctrine
of parity of ministers.

On the other hand, in 1628/29 and again in 1632 he did
find it possible to sign the Three Articles of Religion, as one of
the conditions for taking his degrees at Cambridge: J. Milton
French, ed., *The Life Records of John Milton,* 5 vols. (New
Brunswick, 1949–1958), I, 190–191, 271–272. The second of
the Articles affirms "That the Book of Common Prayer, and of
Ordering of Bishops, Priests, and Deacons containeth in it nothing
contrary to the Word of God, and that it may lawfully so be used":
quoted in David Masson, *The Life of John Milton* (London, 1859–
1880), I (rev. ed., 1881), 217. See also p. 354, on Milton's willingness to "conform" in 1625. Then too we may remember that the
licenser was able to pass *Lycidas* for publication in *Justa Eduardo
King.*

A considerable amount of scholarly opinion interprets Milton's
early Puritanism as moderate in character. Harris Francis Fletcher

has described Milton's father as solidly Anglican, in no sense an extreme type of Puritan. Fletcher explains the elder Milton's "puritanical" leanings by reference to "his friendship with Richard Stock and other rectors and curates of All Hallows Bread Street": *The Intellectual Development of John Milton*, 2 vols. (Urbana, 1956–1961), I, 48. See pp. 48–51 for the full discussion. Fletcher further suggests that it was probably Stock who brought Thomas Young to the attention of Milton's father (I, 59). On the character of Young's Puritanism before and during the Laudian régime, see David Masson, ed., *The Poetical Works of John Milton*, 3 vols. (London, 1874), III, 498–499, n. to Elegy 4, lines 87–104; and Walter MacKellar, ed., *The Latin Poems of John Milton* (New Haven, 1930), p. 215, n. to Elegy 4, lines 87–104.

In a lecture on "Milton in Italy," James Holly Hanford notes that Milton's "grandfather had been a Catholic, his father was an Anglican convert from the faith in which he had been brought up. Milton's own education had not been Puritan in any extreme sense . . . he was as yet no passionate reformer . . .": Reprinted by permission of Duquesne University Press from *AnM*, V (1964), 54. Cf. the comments by George Williamson, who considers it reasonable to suppose that when Milton wrote *Lycidas* he had not taken up the root-and-branch mood: "The Obsequies for Edward King," in *Seventeenth Century Contexts* (Chicago, 1961), pp. 140, 143. See also the following: Arthur Barker, *Milton and the Puritan Dilemma, 1641–1660* (Toronto, 1942), Part I, and p. 347, n. 2; E. S. de Beer, "St. Peter in 'Lycidas,'" *RES*, XXIII (1947), 60–63; and *Complete Prose Works of John Milton* (New Haven, 1953–), I, 3, n. 4; and 822, n. 160 (but cf. p. 108).

For an approach that assumes, per contra, the early and formative influence of radical Puritanism on Milton, see William Haller, *The Rise of Puritanism* (New York, 1938), ch. viii.

32. See, for example, Leon Howard, " 'That Two-Handed Engine' Once More," *HLQ*, XV (1952), 173–184; George Wesley Whiting, "*Lycidas*, the Corrupt Clergy, and the Reformation," in *Milton and This Pendant World* (Austin, 1958), pp. 29–58; Ernest Tuveson, " 'The Pilot of the Galilean Lake' " (above, n. 2).

33. Brightman, *The English Rite*, II, 1017. That *preaching* has always been involved in the Anglican concept of episcopal responsibilities may be illustrated in still another way. A new collect for St. Peter's Day, composed for the 1549 Prayer Book, explicitly petitions for the grace of preaching: "Almightie God, whiche by thy sonne Iesus Christ hast geuen to thy Apostle Sayncte Peter many excellente giftes, and commaundedst him earnestly to fede thy

flocke: make we beseche thee, all byshops and pastors diligently to preache thy holy worde, and the people obedientlye to folowe the same, that they may receyue the croune of euerlasting glorye, through Iesus Christ our Lorde" (Brightman, II, 600). Later on, this collect was given an interesting additional use. In Anglican consecrations for more than a century, the collect for the day was used, since the Ordinal included no proper collect in "The Forme of Consecratyng of an Archebishop or Bishop." The 1661 revisers, however, introduced a proper collect by adapting the collect for St. Peter's Day: "Almighty God, who by thy Son Iesus Christ didst give to thy holy Apostles, many excellent gifts, and didst charge them to feed thy flock; Give grace, we beseech thee, to all Bishops, the Pastours of thy Church, that they may diligently preach thy word, and duly administer the godly discipline thereof; and grant to the people, that they may obediently follow the same, that all may receive the crown of everlasting glory through Jesus Christ our Lord. Amen" (Brightman, II, 999).

34. In 1550 the formula respecting the Bible ended with these words (followed by "through Iesus Christ our Lorde"). Next came the rubric, "Then shall the Archebishop put into his hande, the Pastoral staffe saiyng," and the formula for that action, "Be to the flocke of Christ a shepard, not a wolfe," etc. Brightman, II, 1014.

35. Brightman, II, 1015.

36. The two-handed engine is interpreted as a sword, in one sense or another, by the following scholars listed in Patrides' bibliography (*Milton's Lycidas: The Tradition and the Poem*, p. 241): E. C. Baldwin (1918), Maurice Kelley (1941), Maurice Hussey (1948), Edward S. Le Comte (1950, 1952), Esmond L. Marilla (1952), Leon Howard (1952), R. E. Hughes (1955), John M. Steadman (1956, and see also *N&Q*, VII [1960], 237), George W. Whiting (1958), Thomas B. Stroup (1959), and Mindele C. Treip (1959). The following may also be added: E. S. de Beer, "St. Peter in 'Lycidas'" (above, n. 31); H. Mutschmann, "That Two-Handed Engine at the Door," *N&Q*, II (1955), 515; Byno R. Rhodes, "Milton's 'Two-Handed Engine'" (above, n. 2); Daniel Stempel, "John Knox and Milton's 'Two-Handed Engine'" (above, n. 2); Ernest Tuveson, "'The Pilot of the Galilean Lake'" (above, n. 2).

37. "St. Peter in 'Lycidas,'" p. 62.

38. That is, although the rod of Christ suggested in Matt. xxv.32 obviously implies universal jurisdiction, allusion to it in lines about hireling shepherds will naturally be understood as limiting its

application to them because Christ's rod is the prototype of every bishop's staff.

39. As David S. Berkeley has suggested in "A Possible Biblical Allusion in 'Lycidas,'" 1," *N&Q*, VIII (1961), 178. See n. 4 in essay, "Justice for Lycidas."

40. AV: "Yet once more I shake not the earth only, but also heaven." The New English Bible, used as the source here, is published by Oxford University Press and Cambridge University Press.

41. If, in composing *Lycidas*, Milton really was remembering the epistle to the Hebrews as clearly as seems probable, he would not overlook the eloquent allusion to Jesus that comes almost at the very end of the letter, the final allusion to Him and the only pastoral one in the letter: "Now the God of peace, that brought again from the dead our Lord Jesus, that great shepherd of the sheep . . ." (xiii.20–21).

42. "Smite" (131) is perhaps another such transmutation. Heb. xii.26 has "shake"; but of course one cannot shake the earth—or bad shepherds—with a rod (or with a sword, for that matter). If *Lycidas* 1 and 130 really are echoing Heb. xii.26, and if the two-handed engine is Christ's rod, the sense dictated by the latter may be one of the reasons why "shake" was changed to "smite." For other possible reasons, see n. 19 above.

To return to line 117. I cannot follow Tuveson in his suggestion ("'The Pilot of the Galilean Lake,'" p. 449) that "the shearers feast" alludes to 1 Sam. xxv. In that chapter Nabal does indeed speak of a shearers' feast, and Tuveson quotes v. 11: "Shall I then take my bread, and my water, and my flesh that I have killed for my shearers, and give it unto men, whom I know not whence they be?" The trouble is that neither this nor any other detail in the story truly corresponds with the situation that Milton is imaginatively rendering. Nabal's men would be the worthy guests. Since Nabal himself would be the "host," this unsympathetic character would have to be equated with Christ. But since the churlish Nabal wishes to bar David's men from the feast, he must correspond to the hireling shepherds (i.e., the Anglican bishops, who shove away the worthy bidden guests). Now David's men have become worthy bidden guests, but who has invited them? It can only be Abigail, Nabal's wife (who later marries David). To whom in the situation of the English Church in 1637 does Milton suppose she corresponds? The requisite parallels simply do not exist; and if 1 Sam. xxv is the allusion, Milton's imagination is working chaotically.

Whereas if the allusion is to Matt. xxii, we may easily under-

stand that the masses in the parable of the marriage of the king's
son (the heathen, good and bad, who were invited when Israel,
the bidden guests, proved unworthy) have been identified with
the Christian laity of England, who have themselves been transformed into worthy bidden guests whom the Anglican bishops
(equated with the hireling shepherd of John x and imagined as the
fat sheep of Ezek. xxxiv.20–22) "shove away" from the feast. We
experience no strain at all in understanding the poem just at this
point because Milton has so totally succeeded in imaginatively
fusing ideas about the ecclesiastical situation of England in 1637
with materials from Matt. xxii, John x, and Ezek. xxxiv. The fusion
results from an extraordinarily complex activity of mind, and a
coherent one.

43. Cf. Robert Beum, "The Pastoral Realism in *Lycidas*," *WHR*,
XV (1961), 325–329. In discussing the question of what Milton
had to gain by taking up the pastoral convention, Beum comments
on the *reality* of the pastoral world for him. One reason for that,
surely, would be the pastoral imagery of the Bible, of the Psalms
especially, which his liturgical experiences in youth would have
helped to implant in his imagination. We may remember that
regularly for many years, at school and the University, Milton would
have heard in the *Venite*, "For he is the Lord our God; and we are
the people of his pasture, and the sheep of his hand," and similarly
in the *Jubilate*, ". . . we are his people, and the sheep of his
pasture."

A Poem about Loss

1. This sentence may clarify what was meant by the reference a moment ago to a "turn inward" and to the moral consciousness of Adam and Eve as "the chief *locus* for the dramatic action." I am very far from wishing to deny the thesis that Louis L. Martz has developed in his excellent book, *The Paradise Within: Studies in Vaughan, Traherne, and Milton* (New Haven: Yale University Press, 1964). I should wish indeed to acknowledge an area in which happily my approach to the poem seems possibly analogous to his own. With respect to *Paradise Lost*, Martz emphasizes an Augustinian mode of meditative action by which the narrator imaginatively recovers the vision of lost Paradise; and that, I venture to believe, bears some analogous relation to what I discuss in a following essay, "Miltonic Sensibility in *Paradise Lost*." Still, one wishes to keep a firm grasp on the fact that what Milton is literally focusing upon in the last books of *Paradise Lost* is the action going on in the minds of Adam and Eve. Not, of course, that Martz ever loses sight of the point; see MacCaffrey's admirable review article, "The Meditative Paradigm," *ELH*, XXXII (1965), 388–407, especially pp. 399 and 402.

2. The note of monstrosity has entered early, with the first Homeric simile (I.196–208); and brutish and bestial associations are prominent in the roll-call (I.381–522).

3. II.702–703, 785–787, 810–814, 853–855. Cf. later, the building of the bridge: X.293–298.

4. By two half-lines that he added for the 1674 edition, Milton made still another opportunity to underscore what is in Adam's mind as he resolves to seek some way to

> . . . be quit
> Fairest and easiest of this combrous charge,
> Which I must keep till my appointed day
> Of rendring up, and patiently attend
> My dissolution. *Michael* repli'd . . .
> (XI.548–552)

In the 1667 text the passage concludes with the line, "Of rendring up. *Michael* to him repli'd."

5. Cf. their ways for addressing God and for referring to Him: IV.412–413, 725; V.153–159; VIII.295, 311–314, 357–363, 379–380, 414.

6. Already in Book X the word "loss" has been undergoing some rehabilitation. Along with recurrences of the word in its now familiar senses (374, 574, 752, 929, 1019) we have, as Adam is

being reconciled to Eve, "his anger all he lost" (945), and as he is looking ahead to vengeance on the serpent, "which will be lost/ By death brought on our selves" (1036–1037).

7. On Hell as the world of hate, and on several other topics developed in this essay, illuminating comment appears in Roland Mushat Frye, *God, Man, and Satan: Patterns of Christian Thought and Life in Paradise Lost, Pilgrim's Progress, and the Great Theologians* (Princeton, 1960), pp. 3–91.

8. An innocent-looking idiom that conceals a respectable measure of ironic force. Satan completes this particular arc with another idiom when he reports to his followers that God "hath giv'n up/Both his beloved Man and all his World" (X.488–489).

9. "Ingrate" (97), apt to put us off like so much of the Father's language, can perhaps be defended. Indirectly again, it begins the scene's development of the theme of grace (the predominant word here: eleven times between lines 131 and 401). One can find a tone of voice that will reveal what the word is intended to signify, a mild and pitying observation of prospective fact (see pp. 65, 89–90, 111–114, on the Father's speeches); the denunciatory occurrence of the word comes in Abdiel's indignant first speech to Satan (V.811). The "ingrate" of III.97 finds its balancing moment, and explanation, at VII.512. Cf. Adam's appalling echo, "ingrateful *Eve*," at IX.1164.

10. Cf. the way in which Milton uses the question of Jesus' identity and office as the basis for the dramatic action in *Paradise Regained*. On this point, see Barbara Kiefer Lewalski, *Milton's Brief Epic: The Genre, Meaning, and Art of Paradise Regained* (Providence, 1966), esp. pp. 182–192.

11. Martz, in a comment on what he believes could have been in the poem but is not, felicitously identifies what I think Milton has in fact given us, Adam's "dramatic surprise and relief in finding the bounty of God poured forth again with so great love upon a race so undeserving of this goodness" (*The Paradise Within*, p. 156). That is exactly what comes before us in the long process so elaborately dramatized by means of the encounter between Michael and Adam. Cf. Joseph H. Summers, *The Muse's Method: An Introduction to Paradise Lost* (Cambridge, Mass., 1962), pp. 14, 186–224.

12. Bentley, for example, and J. B. Broadbent, who has lately revived Bentley's judgment, though with some discriminating reservations: *Some Graver Subject. An Essay on Paradise Lost* (London, 1960), pp. 285–286. The interpretation by Frank Kermode, who also quotes Bentley, may be compared with that offered in the

present essay: "Adam Unparadised," in *The Living Milton: Essays by Various Hands,* ed. Frank Kermode (London, 1960), pp. 101–103. See also Dennis H. Burden, *The Logical Epic: A Study of the Argument of Paradise Lost* (London, 1967), pp. 198–201.

13. Henry J. Todd, ed., *The Poetical Works of John Milton,* 2d ed., 7 vols. (London, 1809), IV, 7 (n. to *P.L.* IX.20).

14. Cf. two other essays in this volume, "The Rhythm of *Paradise Lost,* Books XI and XII" and "Miltonic Sensibility in *Paradise Lost.*"

15. When all this has been said, a few spots still remain to puzzle and disappoint us. "Rage" is twice ascribed to good characters, by Abdiel at V.890–892, and by Raphael at VI.635. The Father speaks of Himself as "Th' incensed Deitie" (III.187), a distasteful phrase that Abdiel echoes at V.847; "incenst" is used by the narrator both for Satan (II.707) and for Adam after the fall (IX.1162). Cf. also XII.338–339. The strangest item of all is a statement in which Raphael suggests that God could be subject to fits of temper (VIII.229–236).

16. For comment about Adam's spiritual heroism, see "An Essay for the Tercentenary of *Paradise Lost,*" in this volume. To the details mentioned in that essay about the effects of Milton's change from a ten-book to a twelve-book structure for the poem, a few more general items relevant to the subject of the present essay may be noted here.

At the end of Book VI, with the conclusion of the war in Heaven, we are back where we were at the poem's start. If we reach this stage of the narrative at a point that we can *feel* as the center of the poem, we receive a pleasing sense of wholeness, in a manner of speaking even a certain sense of finality. Then to turn, at such a juncture, from destruction to creation, and thereby to feel that creation is ushering in a whole second half, is bound to affect our response to a story about loss.

Again, in the revised form of the poem the action as it moves ahead seems to take up a far greater length of time. That is an improvement because it increases our sense of the gravity of what is happening. It is one thing to separate the war in Heaven (VI) from the temptation and fall (VIII in 1667) by a single book; a more impressive effect becomes possible if the approach is more leisured, with two whole books intervening (VII and VIII in 1674). Also, the creation story achieves a more majestic effect when it is given a whole book to itself (VII in 1674); its grandeur had been somewhat muted when the narrator rushed on without a pause into what is now the opening of Book VIII.

A similar effect of huddling had been produced (in 1667) when, without the slightest break, the narrator had continued with the story after Michael's heartening assurances about the rainbow. For five successive visions we have been hearing about disasters of growing intensity and scope, the world of death that Adam has brought into this world. Then the Flood itself, seen in the sixth vision, has consummated the gloomy prophecies, for to all appearances it will drown every hope for mankind. How (Adam must be wondering) can the promised Seed now come to bruise the Serpent's head? But then hope is born again in Adam's mind, with the rainbow and Michael's explanation of its meaning. By making provision (in 1674) for a pause at the conclusion of that episode, Milton arranges an opportunity for Adam, and for us, to take our bearings. Adam in the story, and we the readers of the poem, have leisure to think again about the idea of loss. We begin to perceive that loss is something more complex than we had supposed, since it is beginning to involve something more than a simple idea of desolation.

An Essay for the Tercentenary of 'Paradise Lost'

1. *A Preface to Paradise Lost* (London: Oxford University Press, 1942), p. 125.

2. Mention may be made of the well-known study by Arthur E. Barker, "Structural Pattern in *Paradise Lost*," in *Milton: Modern Essays in Criticism*, ed. Arthur E. Barker (New York: Oxford University Press, 1965), pp. 142–155. Barker raises the question, "Is it possible that the simple redivision into twelve books . . . indicates that the process of resolution had not quite clarified itself when Milton published the poem in 1667, that subsequently he saw in it a pattern which the ten-book division tended to obscure?" (p. 146). My own study does not contradict Barker's in any essential way, I believe, though I should prefer not to suggest an imperfect grasp of certain implications and a "subsequent" perception on Milton's part. Recently Louis L. Martz has expressed some preference for the ten-book structure: *The Paradise Within: Studies in Vaughan, Traherne, and Milton* (New Haven, 1964), pp. 132–133, n. 7.

For other comment on differences between the first and second editions, see the following: James Whaler, *Counterpoint and Symbol: An Inquiry into the Rhythm of Milton's Epic Style* (Copenhagen, 1956), ch. vii; Joseph H. Summers, *The Muse's Method: An Introduction to Paradise Lost* (Cambridge, Mass., 1962), ch. v; J. R. Watson, "Divine Providence and the Structure of *Paradise Lost*," *EIC*, XIV (1964), 148–155; John T. Shawcross, "The Balanced Structure of *Paradise Lost*," *SP*, LXII (1965), 696–718, and "The Son in His Ascendance: A Reading of *Paradise Lost*," *MLQ*, XXVII (1966), 388–401. The 1667 text is reprinted in *John Milton's Complete Poetical Works Reproduced in Photographic Facsimile*, ed. Harris Francis Fletcher, 4 vols. (Urbana, 1943–1948), II, 221–634.

3. Two items of contrast at the beginning of these books stand out.

(1) Book X (1667), opening with Adam and Eve reconciled after the scene of prayer that has concluded the preceding book, may remind us that Book V opens as a restless night for Eve is ending with the dawn. Adam comforts her in that scene, but now there is the important difference that both of them need help; and indeed, though they themselves do not yet know it, both have already been receiving prevenient grace (XI.3). The opening scene in Book V eventuates in the great canticle of praise to God (the second of only two occasions in the poem when we actually hear Adam and Eve in prayer), whereas now in Book X (1667 ed.; in 1674, XI.17–

25) the Son acts as priest to intercede for them. At both points, different as they are in general tone, the narrator takes occasion (as he does also at IV.736–738) to comment on the fact that their prayers are innocent of all specious formalism (V.145–152; XI.7–8). For other details, cf. V.129–136, 209–210, with XI.136–139.

(2) The Son's image for their prayers (XI.22–30), reminding us of the care given to actual plants in the corresponding scene (V.20–25, 211–219), may suggest how far we have moved in the story, how much more complex the story has become by virtue of its turn inward, which places the essential *locus* of the poem's action in the mind of Adam and Eve.

4. Some details early in the scenes point up the parallels and the contrasts. "*Eve*, now expect great tidings," Adam says when he catches sight of Michael approaching (XI.226); and we remember Raphael's approach:

> Haste hither *Eve*, and worth thy sight behold
> Eastward among those Trees, what glorious shape
> Comes this way moving; seems another Morn
> Ris'n on mid-noon; som great behest from Heav'n
> To us perhaps he brings, and will voutsafe
> This day to be our Guest . . .
>
> (V.308–313)

As Michael is approaching, Adam perceives the unusual turn in the weather, the darkness in the East (XI.203–204. Note also certain other references to the Eastern Gate—XI.190, 118—which had appeared so different when Raphael was arriving.) Then Adam walks out to meet his new guest, more abashedly now (XI.249) than when, "Accompani'd . . . with his own compleat/Perfections," he had greeted Raphael (V.350–360).

5. Which also, of course, happily aligned the poem more obviously with Virgil's epic. Cf. Barker, "Structural Pattern in *Paradise Lost*," pp. 143, 150–151.

6. Some of these resonances may be listed.

(1) The Father, on faith as the *refiner* of human life (XI.63–64). Cf. V.493ff., Raphael's suggestion of Adam's possible advancement, which is itself the good version of what Satan has already perversely suggested to Eve in the dream: V.67–90.

(2) The Father explicitly draws His judgment of men into relation with the way He has already dealt "with peccant Angels" (XI.69–70). The statement may help to remind us of the narrative of the war in Heaven that we have heard in Books V and VI.

(3) A decree by the Father: cf. XI.96 and V.602.

(4) The Son pleads for the unity of all the redeemed (XI.42–44). Cf. the Father's offer of angelic unity under the Son: V.609–611.

(5) Eve's humble gratitude to Adam (XI.169–171). Cf. V.18–19, 28–29, 95.

(6) The "rosie" morning (XI.175). Cf.V.1.

(7) "milde" (XI.286). Cf. V.371, and XI.234–235.

(8) Adam to Michael (XI.296–298). Cf. V.361–362.

(9) Adam looks for "New Laws" (XI.227–228). Cf. Satan's attitude at V.679–681.

7. Early in the third vision we see in quick succession the practitioners of music, metallurgy, and mining (XI.558–573). Hellish associations for all three were set up as far back as Book I, where they were linked as the narrator recounted the building of Pandaemonium (I.700–712). The comprehensiveness of the survey in the fourth vision, and the syntactical pattern natural to such wide perspective, evoke a memory of patterns similarly inspired in that passage of Book II where the fallen angels' diversions in Hell are described. "Part on . . . or in . . . Upon . . . or in . . . Part curb . . . or shun . . . Others . . . Others . . ." So it runs in Book II (528ff.). In XI the pattern goes "Part wield . . . part courb . . . One way a Band select . . . Others . . . others . . ." (643–657). "Part courb the foaming Steed" (XI.643), especially, recalls the earlier "Part curb thir fierie Steeds" (II.531).

We are alert to sense these connections because very early in the sequence we have heard, about Cain, "Whereat hee inlie rag'd" (444), and then those resonant words "deadly pale," "Dismai'd," "envie," "die," "Death," "terrour," "foul," "Horrid," "horrible" (446–465). The whole second vision has been patterned to stimulate important memories. Michael introduces it with "Death thou hast seen/In his first shape on man; but many shapes/Of Death" (466–468) and thereby recalls "The other shape,/If shape it might be call'd that shape had none" (II.666–667). "Grim," "dismal," "dire," "monstrous crew," and "miserie" (469–476) lead up to "Immediately a place/Before his eyes appeard, sad, noysom, dark" (477–478), which begins this particular vision of Hell. "Dire was the tossing, deep the groans, despair/Tended the sick" (489–490), a sight "deform" (494); and again, as at II.672, "over them triumphant Death his Dart/Shook, but delaid to strike" (491–492). The breathless rhetoric constituting the main body of the vision, a list of diseases that bears one down by the sheer weight of its endless multiplicity, closely resembles that of the tremendous passage about

Hell at II.618–628; and the cadence of the last, climactic, line, "Dropsies, and Asthma's, and Joint-racking Rheums" (488), all but duplicates that of its counterpart, *"Gorgons* and *Hydra's,* and *Chimera's* dire" (II.628): ˡ˘ ˉˡ˘ ˡ ˉˡ˘ ˡ

8. Some other details in the Nimrod story are perhaps recalling items in Book VI: on the wish for fame (XII.45–47) cf. VI.-376–385; and on the materials for the tower (XII.40–44) cf. VI.-476–479, 509–515.

9. The Biblical fact that the resurrection occurred on the third day (narrated in the poem at XII.421–423) perhaps helped to suggest that the Son should overcome the rebels in Heaven on the third day of the war (VI.699, 748–749).

10. Cf. XII.490–492, 536, with VI.212–213. The contrast between the two modes of warfare has also been commented on in Barbara Kiefer Lewalski, "Structure and the Symbolism of Vision in Michael's Prophecy, *Paradise Lost,* Books XI–XII," *PQ,* XLII (1963), 33; and B. Rajan, ed., *Paradise Lost, Books I & II* (New York, 1964), pp. xviii–xix.

11. Mason Tung has discussed the dramatic function and thematic import of the scenes with Abdiel in "The Abdiel Episode: A Contextual Reading," *SP,* LXII (1965), 595–609. Tung regards the episode as pivotal in the twelve-book as well as in the ten-book version of the poem: see pp. 602–603, n. 21.

12. The opening of the last speech by Eve (XII.610–614) brings to mind yet another moment in Book V, the very beginning, when Adam has given comfort and reassurance to his wife after her restless dream. Satan had inspired that one, but "God is also in sleep, and Dreams advise" (611); and this correspondence makes one more item among the many that are uniting to produce the harmony at the end.

And of course, other sections of the poem besides Books V and VI are recalled in Book XII. For comment on the relation between Books XII and I, for example, see J. R. Watson, "Divine Providence and the Structure of *Paradise Lost*" (above, n. 2).

13. Cf. XII.24–32, 82–101, with IV.288–340.

14. This is not to deny, of course, that regeneration is a gift of grace. Though God's offer of rescue is always absolutely primary, man does have to appropriate it (to use the theological word); and although it takes grace for man to perform even his responsive action, grace is always preveniently accessible to him.

15. That is one way of formulating what the poem means by "obedience." I have come to suspect that it was a specifically imaginative apprehension of the fact, a genuinely poetic response to

the poem's artistic means, that led Addison to make the statement which has often seemed critically so irrelevant to many of us: "That [great moral] which reigns in Milton is the most universal and most useful that can be imagined. It is, in short, this, that obedience to the will of God makes men happy, and that disobedience makes them miserable." *Criticisms on Paradise Lost,* ed. Albert S. Cook (New York, 1926), p. 154.

16. *The Paradise Within,* p. 159; his complete discussion of the visions and narratives appears on pp. 148–167. Critical interest in the last two books of *Paradise Lost* has been growing in recent years. In addition to Martz's book, the following items may be mentioned: William G. Madsen, "The Idea of Nature in Milton's Poetry," in *Three Studies in the Renaissance: Sidney, Jonson, Milton* (New Haven, 1958), pp. 254–271; F. T. Prince, "On the Last Two Books of 'Paradise Lost,' " *E&S,* XI (1958), 38–52; G. A. Wilkes, *The Thesis of Paradise Lost* (Melbourne, 1961), pp. 37–42; Lawrence A. Sasek, "The Drama of *Paradise Lost,* Books XI and XII," in *Studies in English Renaissance Literature,* ed. Waldo F. McNeir (Baton Rouge, 1962), pp. 181–196; Joseph H. Summers, *The Muse's Method* (above, n. 2), ch. viii; B. A. Wright, *Milton's Paradise Lost* (London, 1962), ch. xii; Barbara Kiefer Lewalski, "Structure and the Symbolism of Vision in Michael's Prophecy, *Paradise Lost,* Books XI–XII" (above, n. 10), pp. 25–35; Berta Moritz-Siebeck, *Untersuchungen zu Miltons Paradise Lost: Interpretation der Beiden Schlussbücher* (Berlin, 1963); H. R. Mac-Callum, "Milton and Sacred History: Books XI and XII of *Paradise Lost,*" in *Essays in English Literature from the Renaissance to the Victorian Age Presented to A. S. P. Woodhouse, 1964,* ed. Millar MacLure and F. W. Watt (Toronto, 1964), pp. 149–168; Robert A. Bryan, "Adam's Tragic Vision in *Paradise Lost,*" *SP,* LXII (1965), 197–214; Mother Mary Christopher Pecheux, O.S.U., "Abraham, Adam, and the Theme of Exile in *Paradise Lost,*" *PMLA,* LXXX (1965), 365–371; Arnold Stein, "The Paradise Within and the Paradise Without" (review article on Martz, *The Paradise Within*), *MLQ,* XXVI (1965), 597–600; Larry S. Champion, "The Conclusion of *Paradise Lost* — A Reconsideration," *CE,* XXVII (1966), 384–394; Virginia R. Mollenkott, "The Cycle of Sins in *Paradise Lost,* Book XI," *MLQ,* XXVII (1966), 33–40; Dennis H. Burden, *The Logical Epic: A Study of the Argument of Paradise Lost* (London, 1967), pp. 187–201; Mother Mary Christopher Pecheux, O.S.U., "The Second Adam and the Church in *Paradise Lost,*" *ELH,* XXXIV (1967), 173–187.

17. Cf. a similar comment on one particular passage, XII.285–

314: B. Rajan, *Paradise Lost and the Seventeenth Century Reader* (New York, 1948), pp. 89–91.

18. Especially noticeable, for example, at XI.430–443, 557–573, 639–664, 713–726; and cf. XII.18–21, 56–59, 61–62.

19. Cf. below, n. 22.

20. For some typical expressions of the attitude, see two passages in *The Reason of Church-government urg'd against PRE-LATY*: "It cannot be unknowne . . ." (*Works*, III, 198–199); "ye think by these gaudy glisterings to stirre up the devotion of the rude multitude . . ." (pp. 247–248).

21. This is not to ignore the reflection of Milton's personal antipathy to ritual which he admits into the poem at IV.736–738 and V.144–152 (cf. V.350–357).

22. No doubt this is one major reason for the shift from vision to narrative. It may also help to explain why the literary style in the visions has been adjusted — deliberately, it would seem — to exert a strain on us the listeners (cf. pp. 81–82). Milton knows how to make the most elementary externals of his plot contribute organically to his artistic purposes.

23. See *De Doctrina Christiana*, Bk. I, chs. xvii–xx (*Works*, XV, 342–409).

24. Cf. a comment by Frank Kermode, writing about Books X and XI: "Most criticism of the verse of Book [sic] x and xi amounts to a complaint that it is lacking in sensuousness; but this is founded on a misunderstanding of the poem. *Paradise Lost* must be seen as a whole; and whoever tries to do this will see the propriety of this change of tone, this diminution of *sense* in the texture of the verse." "Adam Unparadised," in *The Living Milton: Essays by Various Hands*, ed. Frank Kermode (London: Routledge & Kegan Paul Ltd., 1960), p. 119.

25. Cf. my two following essays, "The Rhythm of *Paradise Lost*, Books XI and XII" and "Miltonic Sensibility in *Paradise Lost*."

26. Martz, too, has commented that Milton's plan is to show the workings of grace counterbalancing the sinfulness of men; but he believes that the poet has not succeeded in carrying out his plan. "If Milton is to achieve the promised poise of sorrow and joy, his visions of evil must here somehow be matched by his visions of good, as in his earlier books. One cannot argue that the Bible and Christian tradition forced Milton to refuse this counterpoint; the tale of Joseph, the visions of the Second Isaiah, and the long tradition of meditation on the Gospels might have shown a way. Milton, for reasons of his own, chooses to refuse that way." *The Paradise Within*, p. 161.

It is true that references to the power of good are not, in the main, of the kind Martz suggests they might have been. Nevertheless, explicit references there are aplenty (see the citations in my text above), and they amply counterbalance the emphasis on human sinfulness. Also, materials of the kind suggested by Martz would not serve Milton's purpose because they focus on visible reflections, in earth and in man, of the workings of grace, whereas Milton wants rather to illuminate directly the inward, spiritual nature of God's redemptive action. Hence (as I have argued) the spare quality of his diction, and the wonderful vivacity of his rhythm. Through such a combination of means he is trying to suggest, even to image, the real, continuously active — but invisible — vitality of grace.

Albert Cook has commented on a somewhat analogous use of rhythm in *Samson Agonistes*. The play, he says, "is a kind of dramatic *tour de force* because the action of the drama . . . turns on Samson's gradual attunement to the divine will. In this regard Samson is closer in conception to an epic hero than to a dramatic one. His decision to go with the Philistines, rather than to resist them, is both the Peripety and the Recognition in the play. Yet this central turn of the action is unprepared for, unmotivated, in the scenes with Manoah, Dalila, Harapha, and the officer. In fact, the effect of these dialogues is the opposite — to induce him to resist being taken to the festival of Dagon. The gradual stirring in *Samson* of the divine will is as inchoate and indeterminate, as secret, as Christ's realization of his own divinity and resistance to supreme temptation in *Paradise Regained*. Or as the purpose of the Cid and Beowulf, the slow decision of Achilles.

"Milton represents this internal dramatic peripety not in the action, but in the poetry of the play, and particularly in the rhythm, a tremendous poetic feat." *The Classic Line: A Study in Epic Poetry* (Bloomington: Indiana University Press, 1966), pp. 276–277. Cook's discussion of the rhythm of *Samson* continues to p. 281.

The Rhythm of 'Paradise Lost,' Books XI and XII

1. Cf. a comment by Northrop Frye: "The precision of Milton's poetry is aural rather than visual, musical rather than pictorial. When we read, for instance:

> Immediately the mountains huge appear
> Emergent, and their broad bare backs upheave

the mountains cannot be *seen:* it is the ear that must hear in 'emergent' the splash of the water falling from them, and in the long and level monosyllables the clear blue line of the horizon." *Paradise Lost and Selected Poetry and Prose,* ed. Northrop Frye (New York: Holt, Rinehart and Winston, Inc., 1951), p. xxix. Frye is pointing, I believe, to a characteristic instance of Milton's using sound as the medium by which his entire consciousness performs its proper artistic function. The sentence in my own text above may imply that I am thinking not of words considered simply as musical sound, but of musical sound in words as the chief instrument through which for the purpose of making a poem Milton's sensibility perceives, explores, and evaluates any object whatever.

The present essay is not a contribution to the technical understanding of Milton's prosody like the well-known works of Robert Bridges, S. Ernest Sprott, F. T. Prince, James Whaler, Ants Oras, and Robert O. Evans, or like the eagerly anticipated work of Edward Weismiller, who is preparing the material on prosody for the forthcoming Milton Variorum. (See also Weismiller's fine essay on the prosody of *Samson Agonistes,* "The 'Dry' and 'Rugged' Verse," in *The Lyric and Dramatic Milton,* ed. Joseph H. Summers [New York, 1965], pp. 115–152.) Rather, I am attempting merely a description of how Books XI and XII sound when read aloud, a description done very simply in terms of the relations among tempo, volume, semantic and dramatic pattern, and such demonstrable features as line unit, syntax, and the relative length of sentences and verse paragraphs. I hope that by such an approach I have succeeded in avoiding the dangers of mere subjectivism that Christopher Ricks has commented on in *Milton's Grand Style* (Oxford, 1963), pp. 25–26. In any event, it will be clear that I do not believe Milton writes verse of the kind some modern critics have accused him of writing. Sound, for all the beauty he makes with it, does not take precedence over meaning in his poetry. He does not intend us to enjoy his musical effects without reference to precision of dramatic, philosophic, and religious thought. See Postscript, at the end of this volume, n. 17.

2. There may be more than one such exchange, as in 500–554.

3. Not all, because dramatically the sentence is leading into the next vision.

4. The last two lines pick up an echo from the Father at III.333–335; and the paraphrasable substance of the last sentence is obtained through a remarkable conflation of Gen. viii.22 with 2 Pet. iii.5–7, 11–13. Cf. also 1 Pet. iii.19–22 and 2 Pet. ii.5.

5. A notable change in the relations between God and men: cf. VII.570 and XII.48.

6. William G. Madsen has commented on the profundity of Milton's insight into the mystery of the Incarnation: "The Fortunate Fall in *Paradise Lost*," *MLN*, LXXIV (1959), 103–105.

7. Nearly 67 per cent. Front and center vowels together amount to a fraction over 89 per cent of the total.

8. 14.6 per cent back vowels; with the center vowels, nearly 48 per cent of the total.

9. 59+ per cent front vowels; 20+ per cent back vowels, and about the same for center vowels.

Miltonic Sensibility in 'Paradise Lost'

1. The most helpful definition I have ever come across for the difficult word "sensibility" appeared in a (regrettably unfavorable) review by L. C. Knights of C. S. Lewis's *Preface to Paradise Lost*: "that perceptiveness, physical and moral, which nourishes and is nourished by the life of the emotions" ("Milton Again," *Scrutiny*, XI [1942], 146; published by Cambridge University Press). But of course a poet is also concerned with trying to achieve, through language, a vital and coherent organization of his responses; indeed perception, response, and the organizing of responses together make up one complex but single action which a poet, *qua* poet, performs in the medium of language. As soon as terms like those come into a discussion, we have obviously begun to think about imagination as well. Although the two can be but imperfectly separated for the purposes either of theoretical analysis or (as this essay exemplifies) of practical criticism, I attempt to list below a number of helpful studies which, as between sensibility and imagination, seem to me to be weighted, perhaps, toward sensibility as Knights has defined it. The list should be supplemented with another (also logically imperfect), appended to a few paragraphs on Milton's poetic imagination; see n. 11 in Postscript, last essay in this volume.

The modern controversy about Milton with respect to "dissociation of sensibility" is surveyed historically in Chapter 3 of Patrick Murray's recent book, *Milton, The Modern Phase — A Study of Twentieth-century Criticism* (New York, 1967), pp. 31–49. Among the early defenses of Milton's sensibility that were called forth by the strictures of T. S. Eliot and F. R. Leavis, the fullest and best are by Douglas Bush, *Paradise Lost In Our Time: Some Comments* (Ithaca, 1945), chs. i and iv; and Phyllis MacKenzie, "Milton's Visual Imagination: An Answer to T. S. Eliot," *UTQ*, XVI (1946), 17–29. Helpful comment also appears in a number of works by E. M. W. Tillyard: *Milton* (London, 1930); several essays in *The Miltonic Setting Past and Present* (London, 1938), pp. 43–104; "Theology and Emotion in Milton's Poetry," in *Studies in Milton* (London, 1951), pp. 137–168, esp. pp. 137–144; and *Milton*, Supplement to *British Book News*, No. 26 (London, 1952), pp. 33–37. More recently, Christopher Ricks has offered extensive, precise, and concrete analyses in Milton's defense: *Milton's Grand Style* (Oxford, 1963).

Other useful discussions are as follows: Introduction to *The English Poems of John Milton*, ed. Charles Williams (London,

1940), pp. vii–xx — reprinted in James Thorpe, ed., *Milton Criticism: Selections from Four Centuries* (New York, 1950), pp. 252–266; C. S. Lewis, *A Preface to Paradise Lost* (London, 1942), ch. xi; Douglas Bush, *Science and English Poetry: A Historical Sketch, 1590–1950* (New York, 1950), pp. 45–48; M. M. Mahood, *Poetry and Humanism* (New Haven, 1950), ch. vi; Marjorie Hope Nicolson, *The Breaking of the Circle: Studies in the Effect of the "New Science" Upon Seventeenth-Century Poetry*, rev. ed. (New York, 1960), pp. 182–188, and *Science and Imagination* (Ithaca, 1956), pp. 80–109 (Nicolson's earlier essay, "Milton and the Telescope," reprinted from *ELH*, II [1935], 1–32); Arnold Stein, *Answerable Style: Essays on Paradise Lost* (Minneapolis, 1953), pp. 119–162, esp. pp. 142ff.; Don Cameron Allen, "Description as Cosmos: The Visual Image in Paradise Lost," in *The Harmonious Vision: Studies in Milton's Poetry* (Baltimore, 1954), pp. 95–109; F. T. Prince, *The Italian Element in Milton's Verse* (Oxford, 1954), esp. the Introduction, pp. vii–xv; W. B. C. Watkins, *An Anatomy of Milton's Verse* (Baton Rouge, 1955), esp. the first two essays, pp. 3–86; A. S. P. Woodhouse, *Milton the Poet* (Toronto, 1955); Joseph H. Summers, *The Muse's Method: An Introduction to Paradise Lost* (Cambridge, Mass., 1962), pp. 11–31, 138–146; Helen Gardner, *A Reading of Paradise Lost* (Oxford, 1965), ch. ii; Ants Oras, "Darkness Visible — Notes on Milton's Descriptive Procedures in *Paradise Lost*," in . . . *All These To Teach: Essays in Honor of C. A. Robertson*, ed. Robert A. Bryan et al. (Gainesville, 1965), pp. 130–143; Albert Cook, *The Classic Line: A Study in Epic Poetry* (Bloomington, 1966), pp. 281–299.

2. The fullest discussion of the narrator is by Anne Davidson Ferry, in *Milton's Epic Voice: The Narrator in Paradise Lost* (Cambridge, Mass., 1963). See also the following: Louis L. Martz, *The Paradise Within: Studies in Vaughan, Traherne, and Milton* (New Haven, 1964), pp. 105–167; Isabel G. MacCaffrey, "The Meditative Paradigm," *ELH*, XXXII (1965), 388–407, and esp. pp. 399–401; Barbara Kiefer Lewalski, *Milton's Brief Epic: The Genre, Meaning, and Art of Paradise Regained* (Providence, 1966), pp. 325–329; Albert Cook, *The Classic Line* (above, n. 1), ch. vii.

3. Classifying the other two-thirds of the poem as dramatic assumes that all of Raphael's narrative, from V.563 through Book VII, is dramatic speech by Raphael. It is certainly not spoken by the narrator. Also, that a sinless angel is narrating heroic deeds to a sinless man, sitting in the pastoral order of the perfect Garden, is vital to the total poetic effect, just as the serene background of a

royal dinner at Dido's palace is essential to the total effect as Aeneas narrates violent events.

4. Cf. I.2–3 with IX.10–13.

5. In longer passages the pattern recurs again and again: I.670–798, for example, where there are new *allegro* beginnings at 670, 688, 700, 710, 752; or II.466–628, where the volume grows very loud indeed from 618 to 628.

6. Cf. pp. 58–59.

7. The rest of the speech (612–615) goes to the brink of disaster, and perhaps into it, although just possibly one may be able to hear a shudder as the poetic response, a shudder not at a tyrant's threat but at the very real possibility of intolerable loss. Also, there is some point in remembering that we do not hear this speech, with its disagreeable ending, until after we have had the divine action of giving in Book III, and the good angels' celebration of that. Milton's arrangement of the sequential pattern gives us a long time to absorb and grow used to that more attractive representation of the Father.

8. Cf. Irene Samuel, "The Dialogue in Heaven: A Reconsideration of *Paradise Lost*, III.1–417," *PMLA*, LXXII (1957), 603; Arnold Stein, *Answerable Style* (above, n. 1), p. 128; Thomas Kranidas, *The Fierce Equation: A Study in Milton's Decorum* (The Hague, 1965), pp. 130–137.

9. A grin induced, as far as the physical properties of the verse are concerned, by means of a high concentration of front vowels, dentals, and fricatives.

10. A sense of the awful weight of human freedom, a sense of marvel that man is invested with such responsibility, appears (among other places) in the Father's speech at V.233–237.

Postscript

1. Besides the inferences one may draw from the overall tenor of Milton's work, certain explicit statements come to mind: the reply of Michael, for example, to Adam's confession of faith ("This having learnt, thou hast attaind the summe/Of wisdome" — *P.L.* XII.575–576), and Milton's own feeling that his arrangement of Biblical doctrine into theologically systematic form is his "best and richest possession" (Preface to *De Doctrina Christiana: Works,* XIV, 9). Then there are certain statements he makes in discussing his own poetic aspirations, and the course of his early life and studies. In the Preface to Book II of *The Reason of Church-government urg'd against PRELATY*: "That what the greatest and choycest wits of *Athens, Rome,* or modern *Italy,* and those Hebrews of old did for their country, I in my proportion with this over and above of being a Christian, might doe for mine . . ." (*Works,* III, 236). And in *An Apology Against a Pamphlet call'd A Modest Confutation of the Animadversions upon the Remonstrant against Smectymnuus*: "Last of all not in time, but as perfection is last, that care was ever had of me, with my earliest capacity not to be negligently train'd in the precepts of Christian Religion . . ." (*Works,* III, 305). One remembers, too, the religious context Milton provides for the whole of what he writes in *Of Education*: "The end then of Learning is to repair the ruines of our first Parents by regaining to know God aright, and out of that knowledge to love him, to imitate him, to be like him, as we may the neerest by possessing our souls of true vertue, which being united to the heavenly grace of faith makes up the highest perfection" (*Works,* IV, 277). The Preface to Book II of *The Reason of Church-government,* again, contains one of the most revealing of all his statements: "For not to speak of that knowledge that rests in the contemplation of naturall causes and dimensions, which must needs be a lower wisdom, as the object is low, certain it is that he who hath obtain'd in more then the scantest measure to know any thing distinctly of God, and of his true worship, and what is infallibly good and happy in the state of mans life, what in it selfe evil and miserable, though vulgarly not so esteem'd, he that hath obtain'd to know this, the only high valuable wisdom indeed, remembring also that God even to a strictnesse requires the improvment of these his entrusted gifts, cannot but sustain a sorer burden of mind, and more pressing then any supportable toil, or waight, which the body can labour under; how and in what manner he shall dispose and

employ those summes of knowledge and illumination, which God hath sent him into this world to trade with" (*Works*, III, 229).

All these texts (and numerous others noted in the Index to the Columbia edition, s.v. "Wisdom") are helpful when one tries to define Milton's relation to the process by which in certain ways the concept of wisdom was secularized during the Renaissance: see Eugene F. Rice, Jr., *The Renaissance Idea of Wisdom* (Cambridge, Mass., 1958). Milton recognizes different kinds of "wisdom," certainly. In the long run, though, he consistently wishes to bring every kind of wisdom into relation with "the only high valuable wisdom indeed." Of course he knows the distinction between nature and grace; but he never forgets that nature too, equally with grace though at its own proper level, is continuously and most intimately dependent on God. A few words in *Of Education* may illustrate the point: ". . . either by the definite will of God so ruling, or the peculiar sway of nature, which also is Gods working" (*Works*, IV, 276). Ultimately, nothing ever remains for Milton purely "secular" in our sense of the word. To say that in his hierarchy of values he gives first place to the Christian revelation means that he believes every thing, every person, every action is finally to be seen and judged in the light of Christian truth.

Understanding of Milton's exact affiliations within the multifarious strands of Christian thought has been much advanced by C. A. Patrides' recent book, *Milton and the Christian Tradition* (Oxford, 1966).

2. *The Reason of Church-government*, Preface to Bk. II (*Works*, III, 238).

3. Or at least, divine assistance that bears some analogy to rescue: e.g., the sustenance of Jesus' physical vitality without food, and his ability to stand on the tower during the climactic temptation. On the latter, see Barbara Kiefer Lewalski, *Milton's Brief Epic: The Genre, Meaning, and Art of Paradise Regained* (Providence, 1966), pp. 306–307, 315–316. The action of the chorus of angels after the last temptation (IV.581–595) seems more like an actual rescue.

4. This is not to say, of course, that Samson is literally a "Christian" hero (as Adam clearly becomes at the end of *Paradise Lost*). I do believe, however, that Samson is a "spiritual" hero, and that the entire action of the drama is essentially a "spiritual" action. Even the catastrophe off-stage, though obviously physical, is performed as an act of obedience to God's will, in response to His leading; and that, a fact about Samson's spiritual experience, is the

most important point. Whether *Samson Agonistes* is or is not "Christian" tragedy has, of course, been much discussed. For recent expression of some differing perspectives on the question, see two essays in *The Lyric and Dramatic Milton*, ed. Joseph H. Summers (New York, 1965): William G. Madsen, "From Shadowy Types to Truth," pp. 95–114, which refers to much of the scholarship; and Summers' discussion, "The Movements of the Drama," pp. 153–175, with which my interpretation of the play is somewhat more congruent.

5. One important topic that has not been explicit in these pages, though it is assumed everywhere, is the centrality of reason — and the emphasis upon right reason — in the outlook of all Christian humanists, Milton included. On this matter, as on the thought of Christian humanism generally, the work of Douglas Bush is especially helpful. See in particular the following items: *The Renaissance and English Humanism* (Toronto, 1939); "Two Roads to Truth: Science and Religion in the Early Seventeenth Century," *ELH*, VIII (1941), 81–102; *Paradise Lost In Our Time: Some Comments* (Ithaca, 1945), ch. ii; *The Portable Milton* (New York, 1949), pp. 12–16; *Science and English Poetry: A Historical Sketch, 1590–1950* (New York, 1950), pp. 14–19. For a more extended discussion of right reason, see Robert Hoopes, *Right Reason in the English Renaissance* (Cambridge, Mass., 1962). Herschel Baker has traced the historical course of humanism, classical and Christian, in the context of other currents of thought: *The Image of Man: A Study of the Idea of Human Dignity in Classical Antiquity, the Middle Ages, and the Renaissance* (New York, 1961), originally published 1947 under the title *The Dignity of Man*; and *The Wars of Truth: Studies in the Decay of Christian Humanism in the Earlier Seventeenth Century* (Cambridge, Mass., 1952).

6. *Milton the Poet* (Toronto: J. M. Dent & Sons [Canada] Limited, 1955), p. 13. See also the chapter on Milton in Woodhouse's book, *The Poet and His Faith: Religion and Poetry in England from Spenser to Eliot and Auden* (Chicago, 1965), ch. iv.

7. Familiar Letter 7, to Charles Diodati, September 23, 1637 (*Works*, XII, 27).

8. *The Reason of Church-government*, Preface to Bk. II (*Works*, III, 241).

9. Familiar Letter 7 (*Works*, XII, 26). The complete sentence, in Masson's translation, is as follows: "Not with so much labour, as the fables have it, is Ceres said to have sought her daughter Proserpina as it is my habit day and night to seek for this idea of

the beautiful, as for a certain image of supreme beauty, through all the forms and faces of things (for many are the shapes of things divine) and to follow it as it leads me on by some sure traces which I seem to recognize" (*Works*, XII, 27).

10. S. T. Coleridge, *Biographia Literaria*, ed. J. Shawcross, 2 vols. (Oxford: Oxford University Press, 1907), II, 12.

11. Some of the most suggestive comment about Milton's imagination is to be found in critical discussions of his poetic style. Tillyard included an excellent "Note on Milton's Style" in *The Miltonic Setting Past and Present* (London, 1938), pp. 105–140. Good chapters on the subject appear in C. S. Lewis, *A Preface to Paradise Lost* (London, 1942), chs. vi–viii; and B. Rajan, *Paradise Lost and the Seventeenth Century Reader* (New York, 1948), pp. 108–131 (see also pp. 39–52). Two fine essays on Milton's diction should be noted in this connection: Helen Darbishire, "Milton's Poetic Language," *E&S*, X (1957), 31–52; C. L. Wrenn, "The Language of Milton," in *Studies in English Language and Literature Presented to Professor Karl Brunner on the Occasion of His Seventieth Birthday*, ed. Siegfried Korninger (Vienna, 1957), pp. 252–267. Among more recent publications, four are outstanding for precise and concretely detailed discussions of some length: Christopher Ricks, *Milton's Grand Style* (Oxford, 1963); Donald R. Pearce, "The Style of Milton's Epic," *YR*, LII (1963), 427–444; B. Rajan, ed., *Paradise Lost, Books I & II* (New York, 1964), pp. ix–xli; Albert Cook, *The Classic Line: A Study in Epic Poetry* (Bloomington, 1966), ch. vii. A good historical survey of the twentieth-century controversy about Milton's style may be found in Patrick Murray, *Milton: The Modern Phase — A Study of Twentieth-century Criticism* (New York, 1967), ch. ii.

Much to the purpose may also be found in another group of works not confined to the subject of Milton's poetic style: Edward S. Le Comte, *Yet Once More: Verbal and Psychological Pattern in Milton* (New York, 1953); Arnold Stein, *Answerable Style: Essays on Paradise Lost* (Minneapolis, 1953); F. T. Prince, *The Italian Element in Milton's Verse* (Oxford, 1954); Isabel Gamble MacCaffrey, *Paradise Lost as "Myth"* (Cambridge, Mass., 1959); Douglas Bush, *English Literature in the Earlier Seventeenth Century, 1600–1660*, 2d ed. (Oxford, 1962), pp. 403–412; Jackson I. Cope, *The Metaphoric Structure of Paradise Lost* (Baltimore, 1962), esp. chs. iii–v; Thomas Greene, *The Descent from Heaven: A Study in Epic Continuity* (New Haven, 1963), pp. 374–411; B. Rajan, "'Paradise Lost': The Critic and the Historian," *UWR*, I (1965),

42–50; A. Bartlett Giamatti, *The Earthly Paradise and the Renaissance Epic* (Princeton, 1966), ch. vi.

Three important essays about the poetic development of the young Milton should also be mentioned: James Holly Hanford, "The Youth of Milton: An Interpretation of His Early Literary Development," *John Milton Poet and Humanist* (Cleveland, 1966), pp. 1–74 (first pub. 1925); A. S. P. Woodhouse, "Notes on Milton's Early Development," *UTQ*, XIII (1943), 66–101; Louis L. Martz, "The Rising Poet, 1645," in *The Lyric and Dramatic Milton*, ed. Joseph H. Summers (New York, 1965), pp. 3–33.

Much additional comment relevant to the subject of Milton's imagination may be found in items listed in the bibliographical n. 1 in the preceding essay, "Miltonic Sensibility in *Paradise Lost*."

12. For the *Mask*, see the first essay, n. 30; for *Lycidas*, see n. 4 in "Justice for Lycidas," and pp. 47–48.

13. Besides the reminiscences of Ezekiel (i.5–18; viii.3; xi.19; xxxvi.26; xl.2) in the lines referred to in the text, xxxvi.35 perhaps struck Milton's imagination as generally relevant, and a few other verses may have suggested certain local details: Ezek. xxvi.15–21 — cf. *P.L.* XI.760–761; Ezek. xxxvii.5–6, 14 — cf. *P.L.* XI.872.

14. *Virgil*, ed. H. Rushton Fairclough, rev. ed., The Loeb Classical Library, 2 vols. (Cambridge, Mass.: Harvard University Press, 1940), I, 560. Other passages from the *Aeneid* that Milton is probably remembering are I.278–279, 287; VI.787–797.

15. Reprinted with the permission of Charles Scribner's Sons from *The Aeneid of Virgil*, page 170, translated by Rolfe Humphries. Copyright 1951 Charles Scribner's Sons.

Milton's passage reads as follows:

> A Virgin is his Mother, but his Sire
> The Power of the most High; he shall ascend
> The Throne hereditarie, and bound his Reign
> With earths wide bounds, his glory with the Heav'ns.

16. Used with permission of Ginn and Company from *The Complete Works of Shakespeare* edited by George Lyman Kittredge (Boston, 1936).

17. This detail, although a most striking felicity, is in the long run no more than a notably conspicuous example of what may be observed everywhere in Milton's verse: he invariably attends to the requirements of meaning. It has long been objected that musical value, not meaning, dictates the arrangement he gives to words. The judgment, which gained wide acceptance in our time

through the criticism of T. S. Eliot, F. R. Leavis, and Sir Herbert Read, is still a very live idea with some students; see, for a recent example, Russell Fraser, "On Milton's Poetry," *YR*, LVI (1967), 172–196, esp. pp. 191–192. Such a judgment erects a false dichotomy. The Miltonic music (sufficiently praised in these essays, surely) is never meant to be heard at the expense of meaning. Both are always present, and ultimately both are always one. By detailed analysis, recent Miltonic scholarship has been voluminously illustrating the delicate concern for subtlety and precision of meaning that this poet's use of language habitually manifests. See, for example, the work of Darbishire, MacCaffrey, and Rajan, Ricks, and Wrenn referred to above in n. 11, and the essay by Ants Oras, "Darkness Visible — Notes on Milton's Descriptive Procedures in *Paradise Lost*," in . . . *All These To Teach: Essays in Honor of C. A. Robertson*, ed. Robert A. Bryan et al. (Gainesville, 1965), pp. 130–143.

18. With respect to the Bible the principle is amply illustrated in James H. Sims, *The Bible in Milton's Epics* (Gainesville, 1962). For secular literature it is well illustrated in recent books by Greene and Giamatti (above, n. 11).

19. *SatR*, XLII (Jan. 24, 1959), 12–13; reprinted in *How Does A Poem Mean?* (Boston, 1959), pp. 768–772.

20. *The Waste Land*, line 63, in T. S. Eliot, *Collected Poems, 1909–1962* (New York: Harcourt, Brace & World, Inc., 1963), p. 55.

A more complex, and more hypothetical, instance of Milton's capacity through imagination to use links of many kinds may be traced from the phrase "at the door" in *Lycidas* 130. As a rather colloquially vivid expression for the idea "at hand," the phrase hardly needs explanation by reference to a source. Yet one may feel that Leon Howard's reference in this connection to Rev. iii.20 ("Behold, I stand at the door, and knock . . .") gave us a useful lead: " 'That Two-Handed Engine' Once More," *HLQ*, XV (1952), 178. Some speculation from the hint can illuminate the way in which, possibly, Milton's imagination worked in this case.

In the opening chapters of the Apocalypse, Christ is represented as speaking the charge against each of the seven churches in Asia Minor. It seems virtually certain that Milton would be mindful of this Biblical prototype for the lines in which St. Peter, though with so different a tone, expresses vehement disapprobation of certain shortcomings in the practice of the contemporary English Church. If so, a literary imagination like Milton's would hardly overlook some striking similarities of diction and idea between John x (one of his main "sources") and Rev. iii.20; the words "door," "voice," and "hear" occur in both. Other significant items, also, appear in the first three chapters of Revelation: the idea of Christ's authority as supreme judge (pervasively throughout the passage), the opening and shutting of a door in a manner that signifies an eternal judgment (iii.7), keys (of hell and death: i.18), iron (a rod of iron: ii.27). Even the two-edged sword (i.16; ii.12, 16) — although I have urged that it is not the referent in the phrase "that two-handed engine" — may well have stimulated Milton's imagination to draw out the element of duality implicit in the image of the shepherd's rod (itself implicit) in Matt. xxv.32, and to relate that element to other "dualities" in his poem. Cf. above, pp. 167–168, n. 16; and p. 170, n. 30.

In idea, in image, and in diction, all these items suggest affinities with the imagery and thought of *Lycidas* 110–131. And the next verse after "Behold, I stand at the door, and knock" evokes images of Christ, and of sitting in a throne, that might easily have recalled to Milton's memory other passages in the New Testament. Forms related to καθίσαι ("to sit") and θρόνῳ ("throne"), in Rev. iii.21, appear also in Matt. xix.28: ὅταν καθίσῃ ὁ υἱὸς τοῦ ἀνθρώπου ἐπὶ θρόνου δόξης αὐτοῦ ("when the Son of man shall sit in the throne of his glory"; cf. Lk. xxii.30). Here the language is close to that of Matt. xxv.31, Ὅταν δὲ ἔλθῃ ὁ υἱὸς τοῦ ἀνθρώπου ἐν τῇ δόξῃ αὐτοῦ καὶ πάντες οἱ ἄγγελοι μετ' αὐτοῦ, τότε καθίσει ἐπὶ θρόνου δόξης αὐτοῦ ("When the Son of man shall come in his glory, and all the holy angels with him, then shall he sit upon the throne of his glory"). And from this text it is but a step to the verse from which, I believe, Milton developed his image of the two-handed engine: ". . . and he shall separate them one from another, as a shepherd divideth his sheep from the goats" (xxv.32).

It is tempting to suppose that links in diction did as much as anything to fire the poet's imagination here. In any event, if Milton really did work in some such manner as this note suggests, he effected an extraordinary transmutation and fusion of many varied materials.

21. Unpublished dissertation (Harvard, 1953), "Milton's Philosophical View of Nature," p. 130.

Appendix

1. I have not found this word in such standard works as the following: Eilert Ekwall, *The Concise Oxford Dictionary of English Place-Names*, 4th ed. (Oxford, 1960); Eilert Ekwall, *English River-Names* (Oxford, 1928); and relevant volumes among the publications of the English Place-name Society.

Index

203

Index

Index

Kranidas, Thomas: on Milton, 160n3

Lady (*Mask*): importance of dance with father, 3; relationship to Nature, 4, 12; response to Comus, 4; moral attitude of, 10–11, 14, 17; as allegorical image, 13

Le Comte, Edward S.: symbolism in *Lycidas*, 45

Leucothea (*Mask*), 5

Lewalski, Barbara Kiefer, 125

Lewis, C. S.: on *Paradise Lost*, 71, 80

Literis Antiquae Britanniae, De, 139, 146n8

Ludlow *Mask*: purpose of masque form, 3, 6–7; framework of, 4; concept of Nature in, 4–7 *passim*, 9, 12; as drama, 4, 6–7; transformations in, 5; imaginative unity of, 5–6, 11, 18, 134–135; key words of, 7; different versions of, 7–10, 12, 17; Christian imagery in, 9–18 *passim*, 129; Pelagian traits in, 9–10; theme of divine rescue, 13–17 *passim*, 123–125; Biblical references in, 14–15; concept of man, 16. *See also* Comus; Lady; Sabrina; Spirit

Lycidas: theme of divine justice, 21, 26, 127; tonal and tempo patterns in, 23–24, 26; Christian imagery in, 23–27, 31–34, 36–43 *passim*, 48; as drama, 24; structural patterns in, 24–28 *passim*; Biblical references in, 25, 31–34, 36–37, 45–48; imaginative unity in, 27, 132–133; meaning of

"two-handed engine," 31–38, 41–42, 45–48; criticism of English Church, 42–43; emotional responsiveness in, 124–125

Madsen, William G.: on *Lycidas*, 156n1, 158–159n4

Man, concept of: in *Mask*, 16; in *Paradise Lost*, 68, 78, 84, 98, 126–127

Martz, Louis L.: on *Paradise Lost*, 80, 176n1, 177n11, 180n2, 185n26

Mask. See Ludlow *Mask*

Melicertes (*Mask*), 5

Michael (*Paradise Lost*): involvement with Adam, 54–55; narratives of, 71, 72, 80–85 *passim*, 91; tonal and tempo patterns of, 91–103 *passim*; structural patterns of, 92, 97–98

Milton, John: concept of Nature, 3–7 *passim*, 9, 12; influenced by Ovid, 5–6; influenced by Plato, 5–6; imaginative unity in *Mask*, 5–6, 18, 134–135, in *Lycidas*, 27, 132–133, in *Paradise Lost*, 83, 107, 132–135; obedience to genre, 6–7, 49, 135; use of drama, 6–7, 24; influenced by Jonson, 7; use of key words in *Mask*, 7, in *Paradise Lost*, 55, 63–67 *passim*, 73–74, 114; Christian imagery in *Mask*, 9–18 *passim*, 129, in *Lycidas*, 23–27, 31–34, 36–43 *passim*, 48, 129; theme of divine rescue and redemption in *Mask*, 13–17 *passim*, 123–125, in *Paradise Lost*, 53, 58, 73, 116–117, 123–124,

205

Index